THE KEEP IT SIMPLE GUIDE
TO NCAA RECRUITING

KATIE MCGANN

Print: ISBN 978-0-692-75736-9

E-Book: ISBN 978-0-692-87689-3

Edited by Isabelle Anne Abraham

Cover design by Esther Cossum

Interior design by Daria Lacy

For more, visit recruityousports.com

or email recruityousports@gmail.com

Dedication

To my parents, without whom my collegiate career
would not have been possible.

Acknowledgements

My sincere thanks to:

- My family (especially Genny) and friends for their constant support and feedback.

- My NCAA colleagues near and far, especially my mentor Wendy Taylor May, my friend Karina Siam, and my entire UC San Diego family (shout out to the A-Team).

- Isabelle Anne Abraham, my editor extraordinaire who guided me through the process and enabled my voice to shine through https://www.upwork.com/o/profiles/users/_~0176450110df3a4d21/.

- Esther Cossum, for creating an amazing cover design that captured my vision and completely set the tone for the book www.100percentcreative.com.

- Daria Lacy, my fantastic typesetter, who literally enabled my words to take shape on the page. https://www.upwork.com/o/profiles/users/_~01c17d5e02b9a27356.

Contents

A Quick Guide to the Icons
Used in this Book

Throughout the book, you'll see three different graphic symbols that signify a special sidebar topic to pay special attention to. These sidebars will always appear in a gray text box so that they'll be easy to spot.

Time-Out: Just like a coach calling a time-out in a game, Time-Outs signify a pause in the text to either take a deeper dive into a topic or further explore a specific how-to concept.

Tip: A helpful tidbit of information that you should keep in mind as you move through the recruiting process.

Trick: This icon alerts you to a "trade secret" or an easier/better way to do something. It's like having a trick up your sleeve!

Stay Up-to-Date:

In case of tweaks to recruiting rules throughout the year and to get monthly recruiting tips & news, visit www.recruityousports.com and sign up for the Recruit You Newsletter!

1. KNOW: Why Recruit You Is Your #1 Guide to Getting Recruited

If you're reading this right now, it's probably for one reason only: you're trying to figure out how to get recruited for a scholarship to play your sport in college. The problem is that you're not quite sure how to make it happen. Figuring out which college to go to is tricky enough—throw in the recruiting process and now it feels like a total maze!

The number one reason why the recruiting process is so hard for most recruits (and their families) is because it's a total mystery. The recruiting process *is* complicated, but it's *not* rocket science. The trouble is that while there are many people who've taught you how to be good at your sport, no one's really taught you how to get recruited. At this point, all you know is what you've heard from others or seen in the media. In other words, you lack the knowledge about the process. Well guess what? That won't be your problem anymore.

Every chapter in this book is built around a "Know" theme, through which we'll get into the who, what, where, when, why, and how of every aspect of recruiting. By reading this guide, you'll have eliminated the number one problem that most recruits face during the recruiting process: a lack of knowledge. And like they say, "Knowledge is power."

The other reason why the recruiting process can be difficult is because too often, people buy into the ultimate recruiting myth: "If I'm good enough, coaches will 'discover' me." The truth is that being good enough *isn't* good enough. Very few recruits "just get discovered" and end up at their dream school. That's why I titled this book *Recruit You*, because at the end of the day, you've got to be your own biggest advocate. You have to learn and understand the rules of the game, work the angles, and get your name out there. If you want to play for your dream school, you've got to *Recruit You*!

Now there are plenty of people out there who can give you their two cents about the recruiting process. Here's why *Recruit You* is just plain better.

1. **I got recruited.** At one point, I *was* you—trying to get recruited to realize my dream of playing college basketball. I achieved that dream and played four years of college hoops.

2. **I'm a recruiting rules pro.** For over a decade, I've worked closely with some of the best coaches in the business on recruiting talent, and I speak regularly with recruits and their parents. I am an expert on the ins and outs of NCAA rules and know how this stuff works!

3. **I'm not a coach.** Stay with me here, because this is actually a good thing. While most coaches have your best interest in mind, at the end of the day, your coach has got "skin in the game." This means that for some coaches, it's important for the club's/coach's prestige and reputation to produce recruits who get scholarships and go to big-name schools. But that might not be what's best or even realistic for you. That's why I'm here to give you no-nonsense, unbiased advice on how to get recruited and find the right fit for *you*!

4. **I save you money.** The recruiting process can get very expensive: travel teams, recruiting services, private lessons, etc. Do you really need all that stuff?

Maybe, maybe not. But when you're uninformed or even misinformed, you might not be spending your time and money in a way that gets you the best return on your investment. If you're willing to own your destiny and put in the work, you can control the recruiting process more than you think. You truly can *Recruit You*! I'll equip you with the knowledge to do just that.

5. **I keep it simple.** It's something my dad always told me, and now I'm telling you. We've already determined that the recruiting process tends to get overly complicated and overly expensive. You can spend all the time and money in the world, but if at the end of the day you don't understand the who, what, where, when, why, and how of recruiting, it makes it really hard to make the right choice for *you*. With the "Know" theme for each chapter, I've broken down the recruiting process into easy-to-understand concepts so that you, too, can keep it simple!

With my experience as a college student-athlete and, more importantly, my insight from working in college athletics, I plan to arm you with the know-how needed to navigate the recruiting process. My goal is to help you and your family make the best, most informed decision for your future as a college student and hopefully as a college student-athlete.

2. KNOW: The Dos and Don'ts of Your Role as a Parent

Parents, this chapter's all about you. Before we go any further down the recruiting road, I want to make sure that we get off on the right foot. Let's touch base on your role in this whole process. As parents, I sincerely hope that you take an active part in helping your child through the recruiting maze, because deciding where they'll go to college should definitely be a family decision. But keep in mind that at the end of the day, it's not about you! No matter how much you want it for your child, or how many coaches you call on their behalf, you're not the one being recruited and you're not the one who'll be at practice every day. That being said, here are a few dos and don'ts when it comes to helping your child through the recruiting process:

DO... goal/priority-setting exercises with your child (more on this in Chapter 6). Not only is this a good life skill to learn, but it'll also give you both a chance to figure out what your child wants. Now I know I just said that "it's not about you," but I'm not naive about the fact that we're talking about 14 to 18-year-old teenagers here. The reality is that they aren't always going to be thinking about the big picture when it comes to goal setting. As the adult, you can help your child consider bigger picture values—things that go beyond just what might be "cool"—such as the importance of education. I also understand that your goal for your child may be to get an athletic scholarship because it's a way (for some, maybe the only way) to afford college. As long as you keep the ultimate well-being of your child in mind, that's perfectly okay.

DON'T... let your sports glory days (or maybe lack thereof) be a motivation for your child to play college sports. If your child is showing signs of not being committed to playing in college, explore that with them to make sure that they're making the right decision. If they don't want it enough on their own, you're probably wasting your time.

DO... help manage expectations. After going through the goal/priority-setting exercises with your child, it'll likely be necessary to do a little expectation management. It's great to dream big, but you and your child also have to be realistic. Parents, you know that you aren't always a reliable judge of your own kid's ability level, so seeking input from qualified outsiders becomes critical. Find people that you can trust to give you and your child an honest assessment of their athletic talent. Be cautious when it comes to paid advice. Schedule a meeting with the high school guidance counselor to talk over your child's academic situation, and make sure that they know about your child's goal to play college athletics.

DON'T... make every phone call and write every email for your child. No matter how much you try to disguise it, the coaches know that it's you and not your son or daughter who wrote that email! In fact, the harder you try to disguise it, the more obvious it gets. Trust me, coaches have read plenty to know the difference! And, if a coach gets the feeling that you as the parent are going to be a pain, it'll be a red flag.

DO... help your child make a schedule to keep on track, practice mock phone calls to coaches with them, and read over their email drafts. For any high schooler—even one who's super gung ho—the recruiting process feels like homework. Hold them accountable and help them create a schedule, but don't do everything for them. Recruits that can handle themselves win points with coaches because it shows that they know how to take initiative!

DO... allow (and sometimes force) your child to engage in activities outside of their primary sport. Increasingly, kids are specializing in a specific sport at a younger and younger age. While on the one hand that might mean more time for them to develop their talents, on the other hand it can easily lead to *burnout*. By the time they get to college, some of these kids have dedicated their lives to their sport since the age of five. It's no wonder that once they get to college and finally have a bit of freedom, they decide to walk away from their sport to see how the other half—non-student-athletes—lives.

DON'T... think that a recruiting service is the answer to all your needs. Don't get me wrong, recruiting services can have their time and place; but, before cutting them a check, make sure that you understand what they are and, more importantly, aren't doing for you. College coaches constantly receive single-paged bio sheets of prospective student-athletes from recruiting services who say that John or Sarah would be a "great fit" for their school. Almost every single one ends up in the recycle bin.

DO... spend time on your child's development as a complete person, not just as an athlete. Even though coaches are recruiting athletic talent, many will tell you that they're looking for more than just someone who can play. They want leaders—young men and women with grit who are mentally tough, resilient, coachable, hardworking, well rounded, and sportsmanlike. These are critical life skills that are often left by the wayside but that make a *big* difference in a coach's eye.

DO... be your child's cheerleader and tell them how much you enjoy watching them play. Your support is invaluable to them.

DON'T... try to be your child's agent. Of course you want them to end up at the school that's the best fit for them, and maybe your family's goal (notice that I didn't say "your" goal) is that your son or daughter plays at the highest level and gets the most scholarship money possible. That's totally fine, but don't try to game the system by thinking that you'll outsmart the coaches who might be recruiting your child. They can see right through the charades and they're better at recruiting than you. Just like we've all been told before: honesty is the best policy… especially since you never know when the winds might change (and in recruiting, they change *a lot*).

DO… keep an open mind and help your son or daughter do the same. Opportunities to play college athletics come in all shapes and sizes (more on this in Chapter 3). Know your goal and be open to the possibilities.

DON'T… ignore the "little guy." This is another way to say keep an open mind. You don't want your child to lose out on what could have been an amazing opportunity simply because they had blinders on to anyone other than the big-name schools, which in reality may never come calling nor be a good fit.

That's it for the dos and don'ts. Now let's get started!

3. KNOW: Your Options

One of the biggest mistakes that you can make in the recruiting process is to not realize how many different options there are to play in college, and maybe even to score an athletic scholarship. Now I'm not saying that there's an opportunity for *everyone*, because the reality is there isn't. What I *am* saying, though, is that there are more options than you probably realize.

Too many people, especially parents and potential recruits, are blind to anything other than a Division I "full ride." This is usually because they are either (a) uninformed or misinformed about the different options; or (b) they're "big timing it" and refuse to seriously consider anything else. But because you are reading *Recruit You*, we can safely say that being uninformed or misinformed will not be your problem. As for "big timing it"—turning your nose up at potential offers from anyone other than what might be considered the top-tier DI schools—it's just a bad, bad idea. Don't let that be you!

You might be thinking, "Well, I am good enough to get a Division I full ride!" That's great if you are; I'm not debating about your talent level. My point is that there are many talented high school athletes out there and, at the end of the day, there just aren't enough spots for all of them on Division I teams. Don't believe me? Keep reading and you'll see why I say keep an open mind.

Time-Out: Big Timing It

"Big timing it" is when someone completely dismisses any interest from a school because they think that they're too good to even give that school a second thought. This usually takes the form of a prospective recruit not bothering to respond to a coach who has shown interest. Many coaches will tell you that "big timing it" is a bad idea. Too often, these recruit hopefuls (and their parents) already start off on the wrong foot: thinking that they're of a higher level than they really are, only to get a harsh dose of reality later.

Bottom line: don't blow a potentially good offer tomorrow by acting immature today! While it's perfectly okay to be upfront with a coach that their program isn't what you're looking for, never blow off a coach by not returning their email or phone call. Coaches talk to one another more than you might think, so if you're rude or dismissive, the word will get around. Plus, you never know what might develop down the road, so don't burn bridges and limit your options by "big timing it."

The following chart helps to illustrate the probability of competing in college in just a few of the sports offered at the NCAA level. The chart breaks down the chances of playing a sampling of sports in each of the NCAA divisions. One thing it doesn't show is the chance of playing these sports at the NCAA level *and* getting a scholarship. Note that most of the time, the highest probability of playing a sport in college is *not* at the Division I level.

This chart isn't meant to discourage you; it's simply meant to illustrate why it's so important to not automatically limit yourself to a Division I vision. I do want you to go into this dreaming big—but, at the same time, with eyes wide open. I want you to be educated about the variety of options out

What Are My Chances of Playing in College?*

Sport	High School Athletes	NCAA Athletes	%High School to NCAA	%High School to DI	%High School to DII	%High School to DIII
Baseball	486,567	34,198	7.00%	2.10%	2.20%	2.70%
M. Basketball	541,479	18,697	3.50%	1%	1%	1.40%
W. Basketball	429,504	16,589	3.90%	1.20%	1.10%	1.60%
Football	1,083,617	72,788	6.70%	2.60%	1.80%	2.40%
M. Hockey	35,875	4,071	11.30%	4.60%	0.50%	6.30%
W. Hockey	9,418	2,175	23.10%	9.00%	1.10%	13.10%
M. Lacrosse	108,450	13,165	12.10%	2.90%	2.20%	7.10%
W. Lacrosse	84,785	10,994	13.00%	3.70%	2.50%	6.70%
M. Soccer	432,569	24,477	5.70%	1.30%	1.50%	2.80%
W. Soccer	375,681	26,995	7.20%	2.40%	1.90%	2.90%
Softball	364,103	19,628	5.40%	1.70%	1.60%	2.10%
M. Track	578,632	28,177	4.90%	1.90%	1.20%	1.70%
W. Track	478,726	28,797	6.00%	2.70%	1.50%	1.80%
W. Volleyball	432,176	17,026	3.90%	1.20%	1.20%	1.60%

* Estimated Probability of Competing in College Athletics," accessed October 18, 2016, http://www.ncaa.org/about/resources/research/estimated-probability-competing-college-athletics.

there that can help you to achieve your goal. Hopefully I've piqued your interest enough so that you'll read a brief overview about what each of your options look like...

NCAA Divisions Explained[1]

- NCAA Division I: Considered the highest level of intercollegiate competition, DI offers the most athletics aid. However, this doesn't mean you should automatically presume that every Division I school's team is better than every Division II, III, or NAIA team. There are plenty of DII, DIII, and NAIA schools that can beat their Division I counterparts.

  Division I is highly diverse with a mix of small, large, public, private, and religious schools. It includes the large, high-profile, big-budget institutions that you

1 "NCAA Recruiting Facts," NCAA, 2016, accessed October 18, 2016, http://www.ncaa.org/sites/default/files/Recruiting%20Fact%20Sheet%20WEB.pdf.

hear about in the media, but this doesn't mean that there aren't also plenty of smaller schools that you've probably never heard of. The median student enrollment is on the higher side, at close to 10,000. Division I is divided into three subcategories based on football: FBS (Division I-A), FCS (Division I-AA), and Division I Non-Football. There are about 350 DI schools all across the country.

- NCAA Division II: The overall philosophy of Division II is to achieve and maintain a balance between athletics and academics. Division II has a partial scholarship model, meaning that most student-athletes who receive athletic scholarships are not getting full rides (this does not, however, completely rule out that possibility).

  An interesting fact about Division II is that among the three divisions, it provides the highest ratio of access to championships (NCAA post-season) for student-athletes. At the time of writing, there are just over 300 DII members, with schools spanning the entire U.S. Most DII schools have a smaller undergraduate size than Division I, with almost 90% enrolling 8,500 or fewer students; the median undergraduate size is just over 2,500 students (50% have fewer than 2,500). DII is about 50/50 when it comes to public vs. private schools. On average, a Division II school will offer a smaller number of sports compared to Divisions I and III.

- NCAA Division III: As the most academically focused of the divisions, DIII does not offer athletic scholarships. But don't let that discourage you! These schools typically have non-athletics aid that you can qualify for and, in some cases, a significant amount of it. In fact, over 80% of Division III student-athletes

20

receive some sort of merit-based or other institutional aid.

Division III is the largest division, with close to 450 schools, which means that it offers the most opportunities for aspiring student-athletes. Almost 40% of all NCAA student-athletes compete in DIII! While there are DIII schools from coast to coast, the majority of them are located on the East Coast and in the Midwest. The majority of DIII consists of smaller private schools—of the liberal arts and prestigious tech-focused variety (think MIT)—with a median student enrollment of about 1,800.

• NAIA: A completely separate entity from the NCAA, the National Association of Intercollegiate Athletics (NAIA) sponsors national championships in 26 sports for over 60,000 student-athletes! Many people are unaware that the NAIA even exists, or they simply ignore it because it lacks the NCAA brand. Want to know why it shouldn't be disregarded? Well, among the roughly 250 NAIA schools, there are over $500 million dollars in scholarship funds floating around! So, an NAIA school might just be your ticket to a wonderful education, a competitive athletic experience, and a scholarship.[2]

After reading the above, you should now be better informed about the different options for your potential future as a collegiate student-athlete.

---

2   http://www.naia.org/WhyNAIA.dbml?DB_OEM_ID=27900&DB_OEM_ID=27900

4. KNOW: How to Meet Initial Eligibility Requirements

When it comes to playing sports in college, your first hurdle is making sure that you meet initial eligibility requirements.

Academic Eligibility Requirements

Each of the NCAA divisions and the NAIA have a different set of academic eligibility requirements. To give yourself the most options, make sure that you know and understand the basic requirements of each division, and do this early! Waiting until your junior or senior year to figure out what you need to be eligible is generally not advised. Why? Because academic eligibility is based on your *overall* high school performance—not just your last two years when you finally "figured things out." When it comes

Time-Out: Eligibility vs. Admissibility

Remember that NCAA and NAIA academic *eligibility* requirements are completely separate from a school's *admissions* requirements. Just because you meet NCAA initial eligibility requirements does not guarantee that you'll meet a school's admissions requirements—and vice versa. See Chapter 5 for more on admissions requirements. I highly advise working with your high school counselor to help you make sure that you're on track to meet NCAA (or NAIA) academic eligibility requirements, but do not rely solely on your counselor. At the end of the day, it's on you to start early and own your academic eligibility.

to academic eligibility, you don't always get a "do-over," so get educated as early as possible.

The Eligibility Center

In Divisions I and II, your academic eligibility is reviewed by the NCAA Eligibility Center. Division III does not use the Eligibility Center. Typically, you'll register with the NCAA Eligibility Center during your sophomore year. However, I suggest that you visit the Eligibility Center's website[3] sooner than that and explore its resources. The NAIA has its own Eligibility Center.[4] Given the more straightforward nature of NAIA eligibility rules, you don't need to register with the NAIA Eligibility Center unless you know that you're going to attend an NAIA school.

One of the resources that you can find on the NCAA Eligibility Center's website is its annual publication, the *NCAA Guide for the College-Bound Student-Athlete*, which has plenty of useful information. Although I'm going to lay out the main points of academic eligibility in this chapter, I'm not recreating the entire guide, so I recommend a quick review each year to make sure that you've got all the little details of academic eligibility down. The NAIA publishes its own version of the guide, which you can find on the NAIA's website.[5]

Core Courses Explained

In NCAA Divisions I and II, part of your academic eligibility is based on your completion of a certain number of NCAA-approved "core courses"; these are academic, four-year college prep classes in the following areas:

- English

---

3   www.eligibilitycenter.org
4   www.playnaia.org/eligibility-center
5   www.playnaia.org

- Math (Algebra 1 or higher)
- Natural/Physical Sciences
- Social Science
- Foreign Language
- Comparative Religion or Philosophy

Every high school should have a list of approved core courses on the NCAA Eligibility Center website; there's a high school search tool located on the "Resources" tab.[6] Your counseling office should also have this information. Not every class that you take in high school can be used to meet core-course requirements (i.e. physical education, remedial classes, vocational/technical classes such wood shop or auto), even if it's required for you to graduate.

Nontraditional Courses

These days, there are many different ways to take classes and not all of them help you meet NCAA rules. If you're doing anything from the list below, read the *Guide for the College-Bound Student-Athlete* for more information and call the NCAA Eligibility Center to check directly with their staff on how this will or won't impact you meeting the NCAA requirements:

- Online classes
- Recovery classes
- Repeating classes
- Home schooling
- Credit by exam classes—these don't count under NCAA rules

6   https://web3.ncaa.org/hsportal/exec/ hsAction?hsActionSubmit=searchHighSchool

25

- Taking a class somewhere other than your high school

- Independent study classes

- International schooling

- Delaying your college enrollment after graduating

Core-Course GPA Explained

On top of fulfilling core-course requirements, you must also meet certain minimum GPA standards in those core classes in Divisions I and II. The NCAA Eligibility Center calculates your "core-course GPA," and it's pretty straight-forward to figure out:

GPA = Total Quality Points ÷ Total Units of Credit

Quality Points: A=4; B=3; C=2; D=1; F=0

Units of Credit: 1 quarter unit = 0.25 units;

1 trimester unit = 0.34 units;

1 semester unit = 0.50 units;

1 year = 1 unit

For honors or AP courses, check the Eligibility Center's list of approved courses for your high school to see if you get an extra point.

The NAIA uses GPA too, but uses GPA as calculated by your high school on your official transcript.

Test Scores Explained

In Divisions I and II, and for the NAIA, test scores are an important part of your academic eligibility. Both the NCAA and NAIA accept either the SAT or ACT, and your scores are calculated as follows:

- SAT score: Critical Reading + Math

26

- ACT score: English + Math + Reading + Science

NCAA rules allow you to "superscore," meaning that if you took the test more than once, you can use the best score from each section. However, as per NAIA rules, your score must come from a single sitting.

 Time-Out: SAT Changes

In March 2016, the College Board released a new version of the SAT: it's back to being out of 1600 instead of 2400, and the test sections are now named differently. You are also not allowed to combine scores from two different versions of the test for your NCAA/NAIA score. For the "new" test, the NCAA Eligibility Center will use a conversion chart from the College Board to convert your new score into an equivalent "old score." That converted score is what you'll use to make sure that you meet NCAA initial eligibility requirements.

The NAIA is also using the College Board equivalencies, but is making its own adjustments to minimum academic standards. Be on the lookout, though, in case anything changes in the way that the NCAA and NAIA use the new score in the future.

The College Board has a handy SAT Score Converter[*] tool on its website, which allows you to plug in your new scores to get an equivalent "old score."

[*] https://collegereadiness.collegeboard.org/sat/scores/understanding-scores/sat-score-converter

Division I Academic Standards

DI Qualifier – Fully Eligible to Practice, Compete, and Receive Athletics Aid

To be a DI Qualifier right out of high school, you must do *all* of the following:

- Graduate from high school
- Complete 16 core courses as follows:
    - 4 years of English
    - 3 years of Math (Algebra 1 or higher)
    - 2 years of Natural/Physical Science (including 1 year of Lab Science if your high school offers it)
    - 2 years of Social Science
    - 1 extra year of English, Math, OR Natural or Physical Science
    - 4 additional years of English, Math, Natural/Physical Science, Social Studies, foreign language, Comparative Religion, or Philosophy)
- Earn a minimum 2.3 GPA in your core courses
- 10 of your 16 core courses must be completed before you start your seventh semester (senior year), with seven of your 10 core courses coming from English, Math or Natural/Physical Science
- Earn a combined SAT or ACT sum score that matches your core-course GPA on the sliding scale (see the Appendix)

28

If you do not meet all of the requirements for a Qualifier, you fall into one of two categories: Academic Redshirt or Nonqualifier.

DI Academic Redshirt (new category as of August 2016)

These are students who don't meet all the requirements of a Qualifier, but who:

- Graduate from high school

- Complete the 16 core-course requirements (no restriction on timing as there is for a Qualifier)

- Core-course GPA of at least 2.0 (no "locking in" as for a Qualifier)

- Meet the GPA-Test Score sliding scale

What can an Academic Redshirt do?

Time-Out: DI's "Locked In" Grades

August 2016 brought several changes to the DI initial eligibility requirements, including a minimum 2.3 GPA standard. Another new August 2016 change is that the grades you earn in the 10 core courses before your seventh semester (senior year) are "locked in" to your core-course GPA. The grades that you earn in those 10 core classes are used by the Eligibility Center to calculate your core-course GPA, even if you repeat them later. The only way to replace a "locked in" core grade is if you had already taken more than the minimum 10 core classes before your senior year. The Eligibility Center will use your 10 best grades in the core classes to calculate your GPA. Grades in additional core classes will only be used if they improve your GPA.

- They can receive an athletic scholarship and practice in the first semester/quarter, but cannot compete the entire first year. To keep practicing after the first semester/quarter, an Academic Redshirt must pass nine semester hours (eight hours if on the quarter system) in the first semester/quarter.

DI Nonqualifier

These are students who don't meet the Qualifier or Academic Redshirt requirements.

What Can a Nonqualifier Do?

- They can be on the team, but they cannot practice, compete, or receive athletics aid during their entire first year. A Nonqualifier's main focus in the first year is to become academically prepared. Additionally, a Nonqualifier is only allowed three seasons of eligibility (meaning three years to compete) in their sport; everyone else gets four seasons of eligibility. A Nonqualifier can earn back their fourth season of eligibility by completing 80% of their degree before the start of their fifth year of college.

Division II Academic Standards

The NCAA revised the DII academic standards for Qualifiers, Partial Qualifiers, and Non-Qualifiers for students starting college on or after August 1st, 2018. The parts of the rules that changed are in bold and underlined.

- Graduate from high school
- Complete 16 core courses as follows:
  - 3 years of English
  - 2 years of Math (Algebra 1 or higher)

30

- 2 years of Natural/Physical Science (including 1 year of Lab Science if your high school offers it)

- 2 years of Social Science

- 3 additional years of English, Math, or Natural/ Physical Science

- 4 additional years of English, Math, Natural/ Physical Science, Social Science, foreign language, Comparative Religion, or Philosophy

- Earn at least a minimum **2.2 GPA** in your core courses

- **Meet the DII Qualifier Sliding Scale (see Appendix)**

If you do not meet all of the requirements for a Qualifier, you fall into one of two categories: Partial Qualifier or Nonqualifier.

DII Partial Qualifier

These are students who don't meet all the new requirements of a Qualifier, but who:

- Graduate from high school

- Earn a GPA of at least 2.0 in their 16 core courses (same pattern as for Qualifiers)

- **Meet the Partial Qualifier Sliding Scale (see Appendix)**

What Can a Partial Qualifier Do?

- They can practice at their school's home facility and receive an athletic scholarship during their first year. They cannot compete during the first year.

DII Nonqualifier

These are students who don't meet the new Qualifier or Partial Qualifier requirements.

What Can a Nonqualifier Do?

- They can be on the team, but they cannot practice, compete, or receive athletics aid during their entire first year. A Nonqualifier's main focus in the first year is to become academically prepared.

Division III Academic Standards

Unlike Divisions I and II, Division III does not require an academic certification through the NCAA Eligibility Center. Remember that Division III is the most academically focused of the NCAA Divisions and does not allow for athletics aid. If you are admitted as a student at a Division III school, you are academically eligible to practice and compete during your freshman year.

NAIA Academic Standards

The NAIA has its own set of academic eligibility requirements. As an incoming college freshman, you will be fully eligible to practice, compete, and receive an athletic scholarship if you:

- Graduate from high school

- Meet two of the three below requirements:

    - Score a minimum of 970 on the SAT or 18 on the ACT (860 or 16 if took test between March 1, 2016 and April 30, 2019).

    - A minimum overall high school GPA of 2.0 (remember, no calculation required; it's what's listed on your transcript).

32

- Graduate in the top half of your high school class—if your high school does not assign you a rank, your principal must send your rank to the NAIA Eligibility Center via an official letter.

Amateurism

In order to participate in NCAA and NAIA sports, you must be an amateur. When you register with either Eligibility Center, you'll be asked a number of questions about your involvement in the college sport that you plan to participate in. Based on those answers, the Eligibility Center will evaluate your status as an "amateur." Most people have no issue with still being an amateur when they get to college, but if you are doing any of the following before enrolling in college, you should do some additional research into how it might impact your eligibility:

- Accepting prize money – generally this is okay, but in DI the amount of money you collect cannot exceed your actual and necessary expenses. DI tennis has additional limitations.

- Trying out with a professional sports team.

- Entering into a professional sports draft.

- Accepting benefits from a sports agent – this is a big no-no that will cost you your eligibility!

- Entering into an agreement (written or verbal) with a sports agent – also a no-no that will jeopardize your amateur status. DI baseball has some special rules.

Read through the most current *NAIA Guide for the College-Bound Student-Athlete*[7] for things that will jeopardize your amateur status in the NAIA.

---

7   http://www.playnaia.org/d/NAIA_GuidefortheCollegeBoundStudent.pdf.

Delayed Enrollment

If you plan to delay your enrollment in college, you need to take extra precautions to make sure that you understand NCAA rules. Delaying enrollment means that you do not start college as a full-time student right after graduating from high school. Most students graduate in the spring and the first opportunity to enroll as a full-time student is in the fall semester. Generally, there is a one-year grace period for you to not enroll in college.[8] Once you get past that grace period and continue to participate in your sport, you will be penalized by losing a season of eligibility for each year that you continue to delay your enrollment. Make sure to check with the NCAA Eligibility Center on how you might be impacted if you plan to delay your enrollment in college.

---

8   DI tennis has a shorter grace period. You must enroll as a full-time student in the term that immediately follows 6 months after your high school graduation to avoid issues with delayed enrollment.

5. KNOW: How to Be Admissible

The previous chapter was all about how to become eligible. However, eligibility is only half of the equation.

Just because you're *eligible* under NCAA rules at your dream school doesn't mean that you're *admissible* at your dream school. And just because you're admissible at one school doesn't mean that you're admissible at another. Eligibility and admissibility are two very different things and, unlike eligibility requirements—which are the same for the entire division—admissions standards differ between schools.

It's important to find out as early as possible what the admissions criteria is for your top-ranked schools so that you can prepare as much as possible. Even things as seemingly straightforward as your GPA and test scores aren't always so straightforward. Here's a good example:

Let's say that your high school transcript shows you have a 3.2 GPA and two SAT scores of 1200. School A's admissions office says that you have a 2.7 and a 1300. School B's admissions office says that you have a 3.0 and a 1200. *How can that be?*

Well, not all schools calculate GPAs and test scores in the same way for admissions purposes. Some give bonus points for honors classes, some don't. Some calculate your GPA using the freshman year, and some only count your sophomore and junior year grades. Some schools require your test score to be from a single sitting, while others allow you to do what's called "superscoring" (adding up your highest section scores from different test dates for your overall best score).

35

Often, by the time you find out that you don't meet a school's admissions requirements, it's too late to improve on anything. You may be having a great senior year, but if you did poorly during your junior year, it might be too little too late. Or maybe you received Cs in five honors classes during your sophomore year. If your dream school doesn't consider the bonus points, maybe the honor-level Cs aren't really worth it! Instead, maybe it's a smarter option to get As in the non-honor-level classes. On the other hand, even with a lower GPA, maybe the college gives stronger consideration to the fact that you're taking on higher level work.

The bottom line is that there's no one way to calculate GPA, and a higher one isn't always better. You need to get the nitty-gritty details on schools' admissions criteria *early* to allow you to better plan out your four years of high school. Just like with eligibility requirements, let your guidance counselor know early on what your goals are and ask them to help you make sure that you're academically on track.

Admissions Must-Ask Questions:

Below are some important questions that you should ask the admissions office at each school that you're interested in. Don't forget to ask early! In many cases, you can find the answers to these questions through a quick search of the school's admissions website.

Q: How do you calculate my GPA for admissions? What years of high school do you use?

Q: Do you count honors classes and AP classes? Is there a limit on bonus points?

Q: Will summer school be factored into my GPA?

Q: What standardized tests (SAT, ACT, etc.) do you require?

Q: How do you calculate my best test score? Is it based on a single sitting or can I superscore (take the best score from each section at different sittings)?

Q: When are applications due?

Q: When will I find out if I've been admitted?

Q: Do you offer early acceptance?

 Trick

Sometimes, summer school can be a good last-minute GPA boost if you need a little extra bump going into your senior year.

Q: What factors other than GPA and test scores do you consider? What gets the most weight?

Q: Are there additional or special requirements for out-of-state students?

Coach Must-Ask Questions:

Once you get serious about a school, it's also good to ask the coach at the schools that you're interested in some questions about admissions. Some, but certainly not all, schools have slightly different standards for admitting student-athletes. The admissions office isn't going to tell you this over the phone, which is why you'll want to direct those questions at the coach. If you're not someone who's high on a coach's recruiting list, don't ex-

 Tip

Don't let yourself be a victim to "senioritis." When you apply to college, you most likely don't have any senior year grades yet, but that doesn't mean that senior year doesn't matter. Almost every school that you'll apply to will have some sort of academic requirements for you to meet during your senior year. Find out what they are, because if you bomb your senior year, you can easily get your acceptance revoked!

37

pect that the coach is going to get into much detail (if any) with you about admissions—other than what's required of any applicant.

Q: Does the school have any special admissions requirements or standards for student-athletes?

Q: When would I know if I've been accepted?

6. KNOW: Your Goal and Priorities

This chapter is all about figuring out what's important to you. What's your goal?

Your response might be: "To play my sport in college!"

Well, yes, but do you have something specific in mind?

At this point, maybe your goal is very broad and you just want to play at any place where you can get a scholarship. Or, maybe your goal is pretty clear. For instance, you want to earn a full ride to a college in your home state, where you can study journalism. Or, maybe you haven't really thought about it that much. No matter where you are in the process, goal-setting is one of the most important steps. We will talk more about goals in a short while.

Equally as important to the recruiting process as setting your goal is determining your priorities. Figuring out your priorities will help narrow down the types of schools that really suit your goal. Many of your priorities will be factors that any college-bound student should be thinking about; however, you're not just any college-bound student! Unlike your non-athlete friends, you have some very sport-specific factors to consider. Later in the chapter, I will give you a sample priority list. Your task will be to review the list, add priorities of your own, and then rank the priorities based on how important (or unimportant) they are to your decision-making process.

Now there's one more thing before you start goal-setting. Have you ever heard the saying, "You're only ever one injury away from the end of your career"? The reason I bring this up is because you should, as much as possible while researching schools, think about what life at each of the schools would look like if you were not an athlete:

- Do the schools on your list still meet your priorities if you take sports out of the picture?

- If your athletics career ended tomorrow, would you still be happy at that school?

- If your scholarship didn't get renewed the next academic year because of an injury (we'll get into this topic a bit more in Chapter 12), would it be possible for you to stay at that school?

If the answer to any of the questions is "No," it's not necessarily a bad thing—just keep these thoughts in mind as you make decisions.

Your Goal

Figuring out your goal doesn't have to be done right at this moment, and it certainly doesn't mean that once you've set a goal, it can't change. In fact, it's very likely that your goal *will* change as you move through the process. But, you should be thinking about what it is you want, and where you want to be, after you graduate from high school. The goal that you set will be your everyday motivation to do the little things you need to do to get there.

A few goal-setting tips:

- Dream big.

- Be prepared to do the work.

- Let your goal be *your* goal; don't try to achieve someone else's dream or work toward a goal that you think you *should* have. Reflect on your capabilities, both athletic and academic, and what it is that *you* want.

- Don't let other people discourage you or kill your dream. But, be open to feedback and advice on how to realize this dream.

- Don't be afraid to modify your goal.

- Write down your goal and turn it into a picture, if possible. Visually representing a goal can add an extra level of motivation. Then, put it somewhere you can see it!

Goal-Setting Round #1

Write down a draft of your goal (whatever comes to mind first—don't overthink things). Once you have a draft, let's move on to getting to know your priorities. After spending some time on your Priorities List, you'll likely be able to better define your goal. At that point, you can start working on refining your goal in Round #2.

My goal is:

Your Priorities

For any high school student looking at colleges, there are many factors to consider... even more so when you're looking to play college sports. Much like a pros and cons list, you have to think about how important (or unimportant) certain things are to your college experience. As with your goal, expect your priorities to evolve a bit during the process.

Below is a sample Priorities List. To keep things simple, divide your priorities into three main categories: athletic, academic, and other. Do any of them strike you as important? What on this list doesn't matter to you? Anything you didn't even think about before?

41

Priorities List

ATHLETIC	ACADEMIC	OTHER
Playing time	Major – do they have what you want to study & is it doable at the school you're considering?	Campus – are you comfortable walking around and do you like the feel?
Post-season opportunity (conference, national)	Class size – student to faculty ratio	Location – do you like where the school is?
Coaching staff	Academic rankings/reputation – of the school & for your intended major	Weather
Team's chemistry	Academic support resources – tutoring & academic advising	Size – number of people and overall size of campus
Game-day atmosphere	Curriculum – do the classes look interesting? Look at both the major and general education requirements.	Social life
Facilities	Retention and graduation rates	Ability to be involved in other activities, clubs, internships, study abroad programs or research opportunities

Divisional level (DI, DII, DIII, NAIA)	Quality of professors	Greek life – fraternities and sororities
Medical care (doctors, athletic trainers)	Semester v. quarter system – both have their pros & cons	Cost and availability of financial aid
Travel opportunities – does the team travel anywhere interesting or cool?	Contact with faculty – do faculty make themselves available? Are classes primarily taught by faculty or Teaching Assistants (aka TAs)?	Diversity of students
Ability for your family to see games – live or streaming	Impact of athletic commitments on your studies – how much missed class because of sport?	Job placement rates of graduates
Uniforms & "swag"	Time-to-degree – how long will it take to graduate while playing your sport?	Campus housing (aka dorms) & dining halls
Winning team – think about how this relates to your playing time. Is one – winning vs. playing time – more important?	Difficulty level of the school	Type of school – public, private, religious, liberal arts, research-oriented

Priorities Exercise

It's time for you to chart out your own Priorities List:

1.   Turn to a blank Priorities List in the Appendix.

2.   Using the example as a guide, fill out your own Priorities List (you can use some of the example priorities, but the objective is to identify your own).

3.   Come up with a coding system to note your most important priorities, your least important priorities, and those that are just somewhat important. For example, color coding is a good option:

     •   Green = *most* important

     •   Yellow = *moderately* important

     •   Red = *least* important

Remember that you'll probably have to redo this list several times as your priorities change during the process. For that reason, I've included a couple blank Priorities Lists in the Appendix. Keep your most current Priorities List in a visible place as a reminder of what's important to you as you continue on your journey.

Goal-Setting Round #2

Now that you've really thought about what's important to you in choosing a college, let's revisit your goal from Round #1. Are there any changes that you want to make? If not, that's okay! If your goal has become more specific, or has completely changed, write down an updated version below.

My goal is:

_____

Your goal may still continue to change as you go through the process. As with your Priorities List, there is a blank Goal Sheet in the Appendix for you to update whenever you need. And don't forget my last goal-setting tip:

Put your goal somewhere you can see it!

7. KNOW: How to Find a Fit

Congratulations, you now have a goal and know your priorities! These will guide your college search for schools that might be a good fit for you. But where to start?

If you're like many other people, you'll begin your college search by writing down the names of all the schools you've heard of—like the ones on ESPN—because if you've heard of them, then they *must* be good, right? Well, not necessarily and, even if they are great schools, maybe they're not great schools for *you*.

The reality is that other than their mascot, colors, and record for the year, you probably know very little about even the most well-known schools. On the flip side, there will be plenty of schools that you've never heard of and know nothing about. But that's not a bad thing! The key is to keep an open mind; don't add a school to your list simply because you've heard of it, and don't automatically discount one because you haven't heard of it.

Below is a two-step process for putting together what I call your "Shortlist" of potential fits.

Step 1: Do Your Research

This step is all about information gathering. Right now, you don't have to find out everything about a school. You're just trying to identify schools that you like—those that meet your basic "must-haves" (the priorities that you identified in Chapter 6). Deeper level research will happen once you've contacted the coach and know that there's a mutual interest. You don't want to waste a lot of time researching schools when there's no possibility of playing there. Think smarter, not harder.

Here are a few of the best places to start your search:

- The College Board's "College Search" tool[9] – College Search enables you to search for close to 4,000 colleges and universities using an array of criteria (i.e. size, location, type, majors, and even sports), for free. It doesn't let you search based on NCAA division, but it will include that information on the school's profile. The tool also lets you build a college list and do college comparisons.

- U.S. News & World Report College Rankings – In addition to U.S. News & World Report, there are annual rankings put out by Forbes, Time, and Princeton Review—all with their own unique methodology.

- Sports Polls / NCAA and Conference Championships – Check out sports polls to see what colleges

Tip

Sign up for a free profile on the College Board website* so you can save your searches and college lists. Two other really great, free features of a College Board profile include:

"My Calendar," which includes important test dates and application deadlines tailored specifically to the schools on your list.

Email Alerts and Subscriptions, which do the hard work for you by keeping track of deadlines and to-dos. This feature takes some of the guesswork out of it, and automatically sends you email alerts about tests and newsletters designed for each year of your high school career. Both student and parent versions are available.

*www.collegeboard.org

9   https://bigfuture.collegeboard.org/college-search

are consistently ranked at the top of the heap in your sport. Who's winning NCAA and Conference Championships?

- School Websites – Once you've narrowed down your list of schools, start checking out the individual websites (both the university's and the athletic department's site). Do you like what you see? These are just a few things that you should specifically take a look at:

1. Sports – do they actually have your sport?

2. Division – what division do they compete in? Some schools have sports that compete at a higher level than their other sports. This will guide you on knowing which NCAA Eligibility requirements you're going to need to meet.

3. Conference – what conference do they compete in and who else is in it? This will give you an idea of where you'll travel to during the season.

4. Admissions requirements – do you fall within the range?

5. Tuition costs – more about this in Chapter 12; visit the Financial Aid section to look over the "Cost of Attendance" budget.

6. Majors – do they have the subject(s) that you're interested in?

7. Undergraduate enrollment – do you want to be on a big or small campus?

8. Location – how far away is a major airport / train station?

9. How do you feel? Are you excited after exploring the school's website? Can you picture yourself

49

there? While you shouldn't base your decision on the look of a website, at least pay attention to how your gut reacts to each school's online presence.

Step 2: Build a Shortlist

You've done your research, so now it's time to build your first Shortlist. The most important thing to remember is that your Shortlist will change—probably a lot! This is because as you go through the process, your priorities might change. Plus, your whole goal is to play college sports, right? You're also going to have to adjust your list based on whether you're truly good enough to play at these schools. If you are, great, but if you aren't, scratch them off the list. We'll dig into this more in Chapter 9, but for now, start building your first of many Shortlists.

Instructions – Find a blank Shortlist in the Appendix

1. Write down the names of 20 schools that catch your attention and that seem to suit your goal and priorities. Don't add a school to your Shortlist if it doesn't meet at least two to three of your most important priorities. It's okay if you can't come up with 20 right away, but remember that this is the phase where you're casting your net wide, so to speak.

2. For each school on your Shortlist, write down its division (i.e. NAIA, NCAA).

3. Based on the work that you did in Chapter 4, put a "Y" in the Eligible column if you're on track to be eligible at each school. If not, and if you're serious about keeping that school on your list, put an "N" for now and make sure to revisit Chapter 4.

4. Check each school's website for admissions re-quirements to determine if you're at least in the

range of what each school considers. If you're in the range, put a "Y" in the Admissible column. If not, and you're serious about the school, put an "N" for now and then determine if there's a way to get yourself to that level. Plus, remember our discussion in Chapter 5: a coach might be able to help get you into a school when you're below the regular admissions standards. If you're serious about the school, keep it on your list until you've at least talked to the coach.

5. For each school on your Shortlist, find the name of the head coach and write down their contact information. If there's a specific recruiting coordinator listed, put down their name and contact info too.

So now you've got your first Shortlist! As you go through the process and hone in on schools, your Shortlist will probably get even shorter. It certainly is going to change—schools will drop off the list and new ones will be added.

Tip

While you can always keep using pen-and-paper charts to create Shortlists, you can also use other tools like a big dry-erase board, or create an Excel document to store all your information.

8. KNOW: The Basics of Recruiting Rules

If you want to know how to recruit yourself, you first need to know the basic rules of the game. Knowing the most basic recruiting rules means that you'll be able to think *smarter* instead of *harder* when it comes to how you spend your time and where you put your effort to get recruited.

I hear from many frustrated people who spend so much time sending out recruiting information to coaches, but never hear anything back. Even more frustrated are the people who spontaneously show up on a campus to talk to a coach, only to find out that the coach isn't there that day or, even worse, is in the office but isn't allowed to talk to them because of recruiting rules. Some of those frustrations could be avoided just by knowing a few basic things about the recruiting process.

In this chapter, you'll learn:

- The 1st Cardinal Rule of Recruiting (you'll learn the other three in Chapter 9)

- The 5 basic types of recruiting contact

- The 4 recruiting periods

- The basic recruiting rules in each division and sport

The reason these basics are so important to know is because they control whether or not—and to what extent—college coaches can interact with you as a recruit. Knowing what a coach can or cannot do means that you can adjust what you do or don't do (in other words, thinking smarter).

It's also important to realize that though these rules limit what the coaches can do, they don't necessarily limit what *you* can do. At any age, you're always allowed to email or call a coach. As you'll understand in a moment, they might not be able to email or call you back, which is why you need to think smarter about how to get them to notice you! In the next chapter, we'll get into the specifics of when and how to make contact with a coach. This chapter is about learning the recruiting ground rules.

The 1st Cardinal Rule of Recruiting

Whether or not a coach can interact with you is almost always based on your year in school. So, the 1st Cardinal Rule of Recruiting is:

Always, always, *always* identify yourself. You'll do this by telling the coach:

- Your name

- Your year in high school (your high school graduation year)

- The team(s) that you play for and your jersey number (if that applies to your sport)

- Contact information—for both you and your high school/club coaches

By "always," I mean that you should make sure the above information is given to the coach *every single time* you contact them... until the point where you're on a first-name basis with the coach.

Remember that at the beginning of the chapter I told you about the frustrated recruits who never hear back from coaches? A lot of the time, the reason a recruit doesn't hear back from a coach is because they failed to give that coach all of the basics. The coach doesn't have enough information to know whether, according to the rules, they're even allowed to call or email you back. Plus, by not giving the coach this basic information up front, you've made it hard for them to contact you.

While coaches have ways to find out who you are if they really want to, that takes time. Coaches are busy people, and they probably aren't going to make the extra effort to figure out who a mystery recruit is when they don't even know whether the mystery recruit is worth their time. So follow the 1st Cardinal Rule and make it easy for the coach to pick you!

The 5 Basic Types of Recruiting Contact

Every college coach has their own recruiting style. This means that recruits will see all kinds of different recruiting tactics from different coaches. Some coaches email, some text, and some are big on phone calls or even face-to-face visits. While the medium might change, all recruiting interactions boil down to these five general types of contact; and, as you'll see in a minute, each has its own set of rules.

1. Generic, Non-Athletic Written Materials: Coaches can send certain types of "non-recruiting" materials to recruits of any age. These materials include admissions brochures, recruiting questionnaires, camp information/invitations, and NCAA eligibility guides (i.e. the *NCAA Guide for the College-Bound Student-Athlete*).

2. Personalized and Athletic-Related Recruiting Materials: The timing of when a coach can make personalized recruiting contact varies by division, and even by sport. This type of contact includes emails, letters, text messages, and contact through social media.

55

3. Phone Calls: Pretty self-explanatory, but again there are different rules about when coaches can start calling recruits and how often they can do so.

4. In-Person Contact: In-person contact means talking to a coach face to face. There are many different rules related to the types of in-person contact that coaches can and can't have with you as a recruit. This includes off-campus contact (i.e. a home visit), and the two main types of on-campus contact: unofficial and official visits. We'll talk more about unofficial and official visits in Chapter 11, but here are a couple of brief definitions:

   • Unofficial Visit – A visit to a campus that *you* pay for. You can make unofficial visits at any age and for an unlimited number of times. However, there are certain occasions when a coach isn't allowed to have contact with you while you're on campus, so make sure to plan your visits around your sport's recruiting calendar.

NEW RULE ALERT: Division I passed rules in most sports that prohibit unofficial visits with athletics involvement prior to August 1st of junior year – separate rules for Football, Basketball, Lacrosse, M. Hockey & Softball (see recruiting charts in Appendix). This does not mean you cannot still visit schools on your own prior to then, in fact you should, it just means the athletics department and coaches cannot be involved in your visit in any way.

   • Official Visit – A visit to a campus that the *college* pays for. There are different rules in each division, but a school can only bring you on one official visit.

5. Evaluation: An evaluation is when a coach comes to watch you play without actually talking to you.

They'll sit in the stands and observe, but aren't allowed to speak to you. There are rules about when and how often a coach can evaluate recruits.

The 4 Recruiting Periods

Apart from when and how a coach can start having recruiting contact with you, NCAA Divisions I and II sports have additional rules about the times of year when a coach can or can't have face-to-face contact with you. These different periods of time are called "recruiting periods." Here's a quick breakdown of the four recruiting periods and what they mean for college coaches:

1. Contact Period – When a coach can have face-to-face contact with you, either on or off campus.

2. Quiet Period – When a coach can have face-to-face contact with you on campus, but cannot meet with you anywhere off campus.

3. Evaluation Period – When a coach is allowed to go off campus to watch you play or visit your high school to speak with a high school administrator, but they cannot talk to you (face-to-face contact is not allowed). Basically, the coach only gets to watch you at a distance to evaluate your athletic and academic qualifications.

4. Dead Period – When a coach cannot do any evaluations or have any face-to-face contact with you, regardless of whether the contact is on or off campus.

These recruiting periods are not the same for each sport in each division. In fact, Division III doesn't even have recruiting periods. I haven't included a copy of each of the recruiting calendars because they can get a bit overwhelming, and it isn't mission-critical for you to memorize them.

Just remember that every year, the NCAA posts updated recruiting calendars for each Division I and II sport on its website. A simple internet search using the key phrase "NCAA recruiting calendars" will get you to where you need to go. At the very least, I suggest taking a quick look at the NCAA website to get a sense of when the recruiting rules allow for coaches to be out on the recruiting trail.

The Basic Recruiting Rules by Division and Sport

In each division, every sport has its own rules about when coaches can initiate certain recruiting activities (i.e. email, call, text, official visits). Keep in mind that while the rules limit when and how coaches can contact recruits, the rules do not—at the present time—limit when or how *you* can contact coaches. Though a number of sports have recently eliminated a loophole in the rules that allowed a coach to talk to a recruit on the phone at any time if the recruit was the one who placed the call. In the Appendix, you can find recruiting charts that outline the most current rules for each sport in each division. Check out the chart that pertains to your sport in each division. Keep in mind that it's possible that recruiting rules might change slightly from year to year (it's rare, but it can happen). This is why it's a good idea to check the NCAA website every year for any changes to your sport.

Hopefully, you should now have a good understanding of the basic recruiting rules. The next step is to learn how to navigate within these rules to get yourself on a coach's radar.

9. KNOW: How to Recruit Yourself and Use the Rules to your Advantage

For high school students, one of the most puzzling parts of the recruiting process is figuring out when they should be doing what. In this chapter, we'll uncover the nuts and bolts of what you need to do to recruit yourself. We'll take a look at the rules and tools for making the most of the process, as well as a timeline for getting recruited. Plus, we'll discuss answers to some of the most commonly asked recruiting questions so that you're ahead of the game.

The 4 Cardinal Rules of Recruiting: Know Them, Follow Them.

1.   **Always, always, *always* identify yourself.** This one's just a recap because it was introduced in the previous chapter. In all that you do, always tell a coach:

     *   Your name

     *   Your year in high school (your high school graduation year)

     *   The team(s) that you play for and your jersey number (if that applies to your sport)

     *   Contact information—for both you and your high school/club coaches

2.   **Proofread, proofread, proofread!** Beyond spelling and grammar, make sure that you're addressing your correspondence to the right coach at the right school. During the recruiting process, you'll probably reuse several basic letter templates—which is

okay—but make sure that you're not telling a coach how much you'd love to play at a school that's not even the one they coach at. This happens more than you'd imagine, and there's no quicker way to kill your chances at your dream school!

3. **Don't take things too personally.** Recruiting involves rejection… on both sides. You'll probably get told "No thanks" by coaches. And, on the flip side, you might be the one telling them that they're not a good fit. Plenty of coaches don't land their top-choice recruits and even more recruits don't get the offers that they thought they would. However, don't let rejection get you down, because it's just part of the process.

4. **Understand that everyone's experience is different.** Your experience with the recruiting process is going to differ from everyone else's. Just because something worked for one person doesn't mean that it's going to work for you. And, while this book is meant to guide you through the process, recruiting is not an exact science. By that I mean that even if you follow every step exactly, it doesn't guarantee that you'll get the response you want from coaches. Furthermore, not every step may be necessary all of the time. The purpose of *Recruit You* is to help increase your chances of generating interest from coaches and then make the best decision for you.

Recruiting "Toolbox"

There are several basic tools that every recruit should have on hand:

1. Skills – This is a given!

2. Resume – Includes both your athletic and academic achievements. You can find an example in the Appendix.

3. Highlight Clips/Video – Put your highlight clips and videos online, and just send the links to those. Do not send out DVDs! Videos don't need to be fancy, because no amount of terrifically timed music is going to make you any better. Besides, coaches can see right through all the bells and whistles! For a quick highlight video how-to, check out the Time-Out.

4. An Honest Evaluator – You need someone who can give you an honest, knowledge-able, evaluation of your athletic abilities. This person should know about your goal and give you feedback on what you need to do to get there. Parents usu-ally don't count, as they're generally biased. A club coach can be a good option, but make sure that they're giving you advice that's in your best interests.

Tip

If you're a sport that has jersey numbers, make sure your number is easy to see in the video. If you're number isn't visible, or if it's difficult to pick you out on the video, try to add an arrow to point your-self out at the start of the clip. Make it easy to find you!

5. An Advocate – This may or may not be the same person as your evaluator. An advocate is someone who can vouch (put in a good word) for you to college coaches. Having an advocate, ideally one who is well connected, is a good thing. This can be a high school coach, club coach, a recruiting com-pany, etc.

61

6. The *Recruit You* Temperature Gauge – This recruiting tool, found at the end of the chapter, will help you figure out if you're "hot or not." You might be getting tons of material from colleges, but it doesn't necessarily mean that you're on a coach's shortlist. The Temperature Gauge gives you a visual way to measure how highly recruited you are based on the kinds of contact you're getting or not getting.

With your well-stocked toolbox in hand, it's time to explore the biggest mystery of them all: timing.

 Time-Out: Highlight Video How-To

With all the hi-tech video gadgets, apps, and programs out there, you can definitely make a great highlight video on your own. But if that's not your thing, there are plenty of resources that can help create a video for you (at a cost). Here are my suggestions for a solid do-it-yourself highlight video:

- Short and Simple – 5 minutes or less. Don't worry about cool music and special effects.

- Basic Info First: Start with your name, school/team, and jersey number (if applicable), high school graduation year, and contact information.

- Best Foot Forward – Put your best clips at the beginning so that the coaches keep watching.

- Make It Accessible – Create a YouTube channel for yourself and add highlight clips as well as your full highlight video. Send links to the videos in your emails to coaches. Include a link to your athletics resume, which should also be online.

- Variety – Make sure that the clips showcase your full range of skills, not just your "signature move." If you're in a sport that has an offensive and defensive side to the game, make sure that your clips capture both. The coach wants to know that you're a complete package!

- Quality – Today's technology is good enough that you can do it yourself with a device that you probably already own. While it doesn't have to be of cinematic quality, if it's hard to watch, a coach isn't going to watch it!

- Keep It Fresh – Make sure to update your clips and post them as you make them. People used to invest in making one solid highlight video. These days, it's easier and cheaper to update videos or make whole new ones. So, update your videos after each season with a new set of highlights.

- Ask for Help – Ask coaches, teammates, and friends if they have any good footage of you that you can use. They might have caught something at a better angle or even something that you totally missed.

The *Recruit You* Temperature Gauge

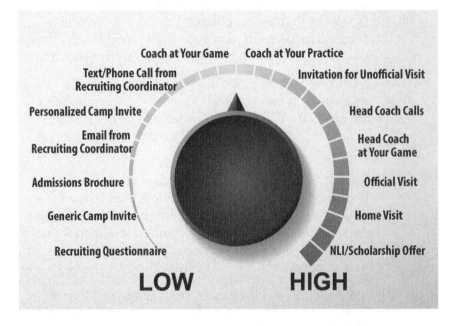

Coach at Your Game   Coach at Your Practice

Text/Phone Call from
Recruiting Coordinator

Invitation for Unofficial Visit

Personalized Camp Invite

Head Coach Calls

Email from
Recruiting Coordinator

Head Coach
at Your Game

Admissions Brochure

Official Visit

Generic Camp Invite

Home Visit

Recruiting Questionnaire

NLI/Scholarship Offer

LOW   HIGH

Look over all the different types of recruiting activity listed on the gauge. The activites on the far left are considered the least aggressive types of recruitment. As you move from left to right across the gauge, the specific recruiting activity is a higher indicator that you're being more heavily recruited.

Two factors that up your recruiting temperature are (1) the involvement of the head coach, and (2) the frequency of contact. Contact with the head coach, in many, but not all cases, indicates a higher level of interest than if only communicating with the recruiting coordinator or other assistant coaches. Also, the more frequently you're receiving signs of interest from a coach, the "hotter" your recruiting prospects.

Keep in mind that NCAA rules restrict when some of these things recruiting activities (i.e. official visits) can occur.

10. KNOW: The Recruiting Timeline

Of all the recruiting questions, one of the most asked is, "When should I be doing what?" The timeline in this chapter will reveal all; it starts off with you initiating first contact, but hopefully you'll also get some coach-initiated contact along the way. If that is the case, you might not need to follow all of the steps for that specific school. This list of to-dos is just a starting point for your contact with coaches. Once you start talking regularly with a coach, the conversation will be more unique to you and not a specific step on the list.

 Time-Out: Early Recruiting

The reality is that for some sports, especially those at the Division I level, the recruiting process is starting earlier and earlier. I'm of the belief that this isn't necessarily a healthy thing—neither for recruits nor for coaches—but that doesn't change the fact that it's happening. Some sports, most notably Division I lacrosse and softball, are starting to take a stand and are trying to limit early contact. In any case, with early recruiting, the same general timeline applies (things have just been sped up). Additionally, some of the recruiting has to be done in accordance with the "gray area" of the rules, because it's happening before certain types of recruiting activities are actually permissible. The important thing to remember is to not commit until *you're* ready. Some coaches will pressure recruits to make an early decision. While you can't put off making a decision for an unreasonable amount of time, you do need to be upfront with coaches who are pressuring you before you're ready, and treat this as a potential red flag.

To-Dos at all Times:

- Work on Your Skills: If you're not getting better, you're only getting worse!

- Do Your Homework: A good player who is *also* a good student has more options. Maximize your options.

- Be Social Media Smart:

  - Email – Get and use an address that's somewhat professional or at least not embarrassingly inappropriate.

  - Privacy Settings – Adjust them so that your accounts are not open for the whole world to see.

  - Think Before You Post, Tweet, or Snap – Coaches do check this stuff. This includes being aware of what message you're sending based on what you "like," "retweet," etc.

- Be Multi-Dimensional: Get (and stay) involved in activities outside of your main sport. Most coaches want well-rounded players and it also helps prevent burnout, which is a big problem these days with year-round sports.

- Ask for Feedback: Ask your current coaches what you can do to improve and if they know of any schools that might be a good fit for you. Ask college coaches what they're looking for in a player and how you might fit into their program. Don't be afraid to ask college coaches what you can do to improve.

- Evaluate Your Coach-Initiated Contact: Whenever you get interest from a school, evaluate how that school fits in with your goal and priorities. Do your

66

Tip

One of the best things that you can do throughout high school to make yourself stand out and to protect your body is strength training. It's not uncommon for freshmen to come in and get injured during their first year because they aren't use to the workload of college athletics. Plus, now you're competing against bigger, stronger players. Starting a strength training program while still in high school will not only put you a step ahead of other recruits, but it will also keep you healthy for the long run.

research and decide whether to add it to your "Shortlist" or to politely decline.

Freshman Year To-Dos

During the Year:

- Create an account with the College Board[10]

- Research schools (see Chapter 7)

- Meet with your high school counselor at the beginning of the year to create an academic plan for meeting NCAA requirements

- Fill out recruiting questionnaires

During the Summer:

- Read the *NCAA Guide for the College-Bound Student-Athlete*[11]

- Attend camps/clinics and participate in summer competitions

---

10   www.collegeboard.org

11   http://www.ncaapublications.com/productdownloads/CBSA19.pdf

- Create your athletics resume

- Create your highlight video

 Time-Out: What's a recruiting questionnaire?

Almost every sport at every school has an online recruiting questionnaire where recruits fill out information (i.e. academic and sports stats, team info, etc.). This information goes into a coach's recruiting database. It doesn't mean that the coach is definitely going to contact you, but it's at least a starting point for getting on a coach's radar. A lot of times, it's a good way to find out about a school's camps or clinics, because coaches often email camp information out to people who are in their database. The questionnaires can typically be found on the website of the athletics department. Fill out (and update as needed) questionnaires for any schools that you're interested in. Looking at the *Recruit You* Temperature Gauge from Chapter 9, you can see that questionnaires are a pretty basic way for a coach to show interest in you. NCAA rules let coaches email or mail you questionnaires at any time regardless of your age.

Sophomore Year To-Dos

During the Year:

- Register with the NCAA Eligibility Center

- SAT/ACT practice (check out the College Board's website[12] for practice exams)

- Start your "Shortlist" (see Chapter 7)

- Check-in meeting with high school guidance counselor; show them your Shortlist

Trick

Registering with the Eligibility Center costs $90[*]. Before you pay the fee, check to see if you qualify for a "Fee Waiver." To qualify, you must have been eligible for a fee waiver for your SAT/ACT exam. Your high school will need to help you with getting the waiver.

[*] The registration fee increases every so often, $90 is the cost as of 2019.

- Email your Shortlist schools (sample emails in the Appendix)

  - #1: Beginning of Year Intro Email

  - #2: Mid-Year Update Email

  - #3: End of Year + Summer Schedule Email

During the Summer:

- Practice an introductory call to a coach – be prepared to leave a voicemail (sample script & dates when coaches can speak with you on phone in each sport in the Appendix)

---

12   www.collegeboard.org

69

- Attend camps/clinics and participate in summer competitions

- Update your resume and highlight video

- Update your Shortlist and send an Intro Email to any new additions

- Plan and make unofficial visits (more of this in Chapter 11)

Remember, if visiting a DI school in sports other than basketball or football, athletics cannot be involved in your unofficial visit until August 1st of junior year (Aug. 8th of soph. year for M. BBall; Sept 1 of junior year for Lax and Softball).

 Time-Out: Camps & Tournaments

College coaches don't attend just any only old camp or tournament to recruit. They are selective about where they spend their time, so you should be too! A lot of camps, clinics, and travel teams are purely run as moneymakers. Just because you received an "invitation" to a camp or travel team doesn't mean that it's what you should do. Talk to knowledgeable people whom you trust and who know your ambitions. Ask them which ones they think will give you the most exposure to the kinds of schools that you're interested in.

Many camps and clinics also publicize the fact that college coaches will be in attendance or are working the event. Attending a camp where a school you're interested in is going to be represented can be a great way to get exposure.

Junior Year To-Dos

During the Year:

- Check-in meeting with high school guidance counselor; show them your Shortlist

- SAT/ACT; have scores sent to the NCAA Eligibility Center (code 9999)

- Determine your family's budget for school and Expected Family Contribution (EFC); we cover this in detail in Chapter 12

Tip

If there's a school that you want to go visit, don't just show up unannounced! Contact the coach, and see if someone from their staff is going to be there and if they'd be willing to meet you. It's okay to still go if you can't talk to them ahead of time; just don't be totally surprised if they're not there when you show up. Coaches are out on the road recruiting, a lot!

- Update your Shortlist

- Email your Shortlist schools (sample emails in the Appendix)

- Phone calls to shortlisted schools/coaches

- Take unofficial visits (during winter or spring break)

- Verbally commit to a college, but only if you're 100% comfortable and know what it means for you and the coach (more on this in Chapter 13)

During the Summer:

- Send your official high school transcripts to the NCAA Eligibility Center

- Retake the SAT/ACT if necessary; send the scores to NCAA Eligibility Center (code 9999)

- Update your Shortlist; focus on your top 10
- Update your highlight video and athletics resume
- Attend camps/tournaments
- Start working on personal statements for school applications

Tip

For many schools, the last acceptable test date for taking the SAT or ACT is in December!

Senior Year To-Dos

During the Year:

- Retake the SAT/ACT if necessary; send the scores to NCAA Eligibility Center (code 9999)

- Check-in meeting with high school guidance counselor

- Update your Shortlist; focus on your top 5

- Submit college applications (use your CollegeBoard.org account to help keep track of deadlines)

- File your FAFSA (more on this in Chapter 12)

- Schedule and make official visits (more on this in Chapter 11)

- After April 1, request your "Final Amateurism Certification" from the NCAA Eligibility Center

- Commit to a college officially, only if you're comfortable and know what it means (more on this in Chapter 13)

- Graduate!

- Send your final official transcripts to the NCAA Eligibility Center

 Trick

Many schools with extreme climates will plan their recruit visits during the best time(s) of the year, possibly giving you a false sense of what it's like all year long. If there's a school that you're interested in, which is located in a climate different from what you're used to, see if you can plan a visit during its "bad" season. Even if you make your official visit during optimal weather season, try to see the campus at least once when the weather is more extreme.

73

Frequently Asked Recruiting Q&As:

Q: How early should I start?

A: It depends on what sport you play. While I generally recommend starting during your freshman year, the reality is that in some sports, the process starts earlier and earlier (think middle school). But this isn't the case for all sports, and the ones that do begin early typically run the most elite programs. If your sport has an earlier recruiting timeline, you can still follow the same steps in the *Recruit You* Recruiting Timeline—just speed up the schedule.

Tip

Depending on when you first initiate contact with a coach, you'll combine your introductory details with a season recap, plus your summer schedule if you know it.

Q: I'm a junior, is it too late for me?

A: No. Coaches never stop recruiting and even when a recruiting class is set, it can all fall apart if a coach changes schools or if a recruit drops out. The general idea is that the earlier you start, the better chance you have of getting your name out there, which hopefully means more options. But, at the end of the day, it isn't over until it's over; there are plenty of stories of recruits who make rosters as walk-on players.

Also, keep in mind the NCAA rules. Some things can't even happen until junior or even senior year. You should understand that different sports have different recruiting cultures—some do most of their recruiting late, while some recruit and try to get kids to commit very early. Personally, I think the trend of committing before junior year is a bad idea. Think of all the life-changing events that can happen in the two years before you graduate! However, that doesn't mean that you shouldn't commit early if it's right for you. More on commitments in Chapter 13.

Q: Are there any other tricks for having contact with coaches before it's permissible for them to contact me?

A: Depends. In some sports, college coaches are allowed to work with local club teams that have prospect-aged players if those players live within a certain distance from the campus. This gives you a major opportunity to get to know the coaches. Camps and clinics are another way to get an inside look at a school and a coach's style. Most contact that happens with college coaches, before it becomes permissible for them to initiate contact, is through recruit-initiated contact and through club/high school coaches.

Q: How do I know if I'm a top recruit or not?

A: Take your recruiting temperature using the *Recruit You* Temperature Gauge from Chapter 9.

Q: Should I commit early?

A: It depends. The two most important things when it comes to committing are to make sure that 1) you understand what it means, and 2) you're comfortable with your decision. While some coaches can and do move fast, if a coach is pressuring you to make a decision before you're ready, that might be a red flag. More about this in Chapter 13.

Q: Should I use a recruiting service?

A: This also depends. Recruiting services aren't going to be the answer to all of your prayers. Plus, they're expensive! However, many of them do have some free resources that are worth a look. At the end of the day, you need to do your homework and find out exactly what the recruiting service is going to do for you before paying them a cent. Many of the coaches that I talk to caution against them. All that money might be better spent playing for a better club, traveling to a high-exposure tournament, or signing up for an elite college camp. You and your family need to figure out where you'll get the best bang for your buck. Consult your coaches, mentors, and advocates.

Q: You said in Chapter 8 that a coach can't call me until such and such date, but I got a call from them last week… how does that work?

A: As with any industry or organization, sometimes rules get broken. Most of the time, coaches break recruiting rules by accident. There are many rules and coaches are out talking to many people, so mistakes can happen. But, there are some coaches that intentionally break a rule. If such a coach contacts you before it's permissible for them to do so, be on your guard. I am not saying that they're a bad person or that you shouldn't go to their school; however, I am suggesting that when making your final decision, consider whether or not this is the kind of coach that you want to play for.

11. KNOW: What to Do on Campus Visits — Official and Unofficial Visits

Campus visits are an important part of the recruiting process. Visiting a school gives you a real feel for the campus, the city or town, the weather, the coach, and the team. You can do all the online research you want, but there's no substitute for the real thing!

NCAA rules divide campus visits into two categories: "official visits" and "unofficial visits." The NAIA does not have any rules regarding campus visits. Now let's take a look at the NCAA's two categories.

What's the Difference?

Cost: Official visits are paid in part or whole by the school. This means that they can pay for your travel, lodging, food, and reasonable entertainment while you're on your visit. Plus, the coach can provide you with complimentary tickets to a home game that takes place during your visit. Unofficial visits are paid for by you. The school might still give you complimentary tickets to a home game, but all the other costs are to be covered by you.

Number: You are only allowed to go on *one* official visit to each school. In DI, there's also a limit on the total number of official visits that you can make to any DI schools: five. You can make an unlimited number of unofficial visits. See the end of chapter for special D1 men's basketball rules.

Timing: There are strict rules in each NCAA Division regarding when you can go on official visits. Making unofficial visits, on the other hand, is pretty easy. Apart from a few exceptions, you can pretty much make unofficial visits at any time and at any age. However, in 2018, Division I passed a new rule that says in sports other than football and basketball, an unofficial visit with athletics involvement cannot occur prior to September 1st of junior year. (Aug 1st of soph. year for D1 MBB). This means that while you can, and should visit a school before junior year, the coach or athletics department cannot be part of the visit. Below is a breakdown of the dates for your first opportunity to make official visits in each division:

- **DI: August 1st of junior year in all sports except Sept. 1st of junior year for Baseball, Lax & Softball. W. Basketball & Football have special rules (see Recruiting Rules charts in Appendix).**

- DII: June 15 going into junior year

- DIII: January 1 of junior year

Length: Official visits are typically longer visits because schools are allowed to host you for up to 48 hours. Usually, you'll be paired up with a current student-athlete on the team and shadow them for two days: staying in the dorms, eating with the team, maybe going to a class, and watching a practice and/or a home game. It's a real inside look at what it's like to be a student-athlete at that school. During an official visit, it's likely that you'll also have a meeting with the head coach to talk about where you are in the recruiting process.

Unofficial visits don't have a set time limit because the school can't pay for much of anything. They usually last a few hours or, at most, a day. Typical things to expect on an unofficial visit are a campus tour, a tour of the athletics facilities, and a meeting with a coach. You might be able to watch a practice or catch a home game, depending on when you visit.

Invitation: Official visits are arranged by the coach inviting you; you can't just show up uninvited! But, what you can do is initiate a conversation about an official visit with a coach. For example, if you're in the second semester of your junior year, and you've been having regular, encouraging contact with a school but an official visit hasn't come up in conversation, it's okay to ask the coach the following:

> "Coach, I'm trying to plan things out for making my decision next year, and you're one of my top choices. I wanted to see if you're planning to have me come on an official visit."

It's better to be up front than to keep wasting your time.

Unofficial visits can be initiated by either you or the coach.

Recruiting Temperature: An official visit invitation means that you're one of the school's top recruits. For unofficial visits, it depends. If you initiated things yourself, it's hard to say, but I wouldn't put too much stock in it. If the coach invited you on the unofficial visit, this is a stronger indicator that you're in the mix for their recruiting class—they want to know more about you. Pay close attention to the timing and type of contact that you receive from the coaches right after a visit to get an idea of how things went. On both official and unofficial visits, you're likely to have a meeting with the coach to talk about where you stand. On unofficial visits, it might not be the head coach that you talk to. Use those meetings to ask questions and get feedback.

What to Watch: When you're on campus visits, you'll get an up close and personal chance to see what it's like to be a student-athlete in the program. Don't just watch things happen; watch with a purpose! Here's what I mean:

> Practice or Game Day: You might have an opportunity to watch practice or even be there for game day. Pay attention to how the coach talks to the players

and how the players interact with one another. Do you like the team's style of play? Do you like their coaching style in practice or during the game? What's the game-day atmosphere like?

Classes: On some visits, the recruit goes to a class or two with a student-athlete host. You can't base everything off what you see on the visit, but what kind of academic culture do you observe? Do the players actually go to class? Do they pay attention? Where do they sit? Some coaches have a rule that they have to sit in the first two rows. Do the coaches have to check that the players are going to class? Are there resources (advisors/tutors) for the student-athletes if they need help?

Observing how your potential teammates handle their studies can give you insight into how the players and coaches prioritize school. You might need a school that has more built-in structure and accountability. Perhaps you want a highly academic school. Keep your eyes open to clues about whether or not the school is what you're looking for academically.

Tip

Keep in mind how you present yourself during any campus visit. As much as campus visits are about you figuring out if a school is the right fit for you, it's just as much about the coach figuring out if you're the right fit for them! This also goes for how you interact with the student-athletes. They'll probably relay information about you to the coaches, and are feeling you out too.

Questions: Campus visits are a good time for deeper questions—things that are difficult to ask and answer in an email. Make sure to have some questions that aren't just "Googleable." Those kinds of basic questions are alright if you're on an unofficial visit early in the process. However, it's better to figure those out yourself by doing your research before a visit. Why? Doing your research shows that you're informed, which in turn shows the coach that you're genuinely interested in their program.

In addition to questions for the coaches, it's important to have some questions for your potential future teammates. It's one of the few times that you'll get such direct contact with them, as most of the time you'll be communicating with the coaches. There's no one better to ask what it's *really* like to be a student-athlete at the school than the student-athletes who are already there!

Here are some sample questions to ask on campus visits:

Questions for your potential future teammates (in no particular order):

- How do you like going to school here?

- How do you like playing for coach?

- Why did you choose to come here?

- Is coach the same once you get here as he/she is during recruitment?

- How are classes?

- What's it like having to balance school and sports?

- What's it like being on the team? Do people hang out much outside of practice?

- What's the social life like here?

- Do sports impact what major you pick? Will I be able to major in what I want and play here?

- What kind of academic help is available if I'm having trouble in classes?

- What's the best part of going to school here? What's the hardest?

- What's game day like?

- How do you like living on campus?

Questions to ask the coach:

- Where do you see me fitting into the roster/lineup?

- Are you considering me for a scholarship?

- Is there anything else I need to do to meet admissions requirements / eligibility rules?

- Is there anything else I need to do to secure a roster spot with you?

- How long does it take most players to graduate?

- What skills do I still need to work on to compete for play-ing time next year?

- Will I be able to major in what I want and play here?

- What kind of academic help is available if I'm having trouble in classes?

Questions to ask yourself:

- How do I feel being on cam-pus?

- Do I feel comfortable with coach?

- Do I feel comfortable with my potential teammates?

 Trick

Before an official visit, ask the coach to send you an itiner-ary if they haven't already. If a meeting with an academic advisor isn't on the list, ask for one. While you're on the trip, talk to the advisor about what a potential graduation plan might look like with your sport and the major that you're considering.

- Would I like being a student here, even if I didn't play my sport?

Questions to be prepared to answer (you might get asked by the coach):

- What other schools are you looking at?

- What other schools have you visited or plan to visit?

- Are you ready to commit at this point?

New Rule Alert: D1 men's basketball rules now allow a recruit to take more than 1 official visit to a specific school and more than 5 total official visits while in high school. Men's basketball recruits can take a total of 5 official visits to D1 schools during their junior year and another 5 visits during senior year. This includes being able to visit the same school for an official visit in both their junior and senior years.

12. KNOW: The Costs —
Financial Aid 101 (Parents,
this one's written for you!)

Disclaimer: Let me stress that this book should not be your only reference on financial aid and how to afford college. Both federal regulations and NCAA rules regarding financial aid are always evolving. My goal is to give you some basics and an understanding of how athletic scholarships work. If possible, your family should meet with a financial advisor and do additional research, including visiting the government's official FAFSA website.[13]

We all know that college is not cheap. While an athletic scholarship (or other types of scholarships when considering DIII) are a big help, the reality is that college can be the single biggest expense for a family. With that in mind, it's important to understand the different types of aid available and key financial aid terminology, as well as what getting an athletic scholarship does, and doesn't, mean.

The Basic Types of Aid:

* Scholarships: Money you don't have to pay back. Athletic scholarships fall into this category, as do scholarships available through schools and outside agencies. Search the Internet for as many scholarship opportunities as possible. Don't really think that there are any scholarships available? As part of my job in college athletics, I see students get the most random of scholarships. There's money out there!

  Many scholarships are available through local chapters of national organizations, such as Rotary Inter-

---

13   www.fafsa.ed.gov

national and Kiwanis International. Other than just "Googling" scholarships using keywords (e.g. race, gender, ethnicity, town, sport, majors, etc.), I suggest finding out if your city/town has a scholarship foundation, calling your local government offices to inquire about local scholarships, and using online tools like Fastweb.[14]

- Grants: Also money that doesn't need to be paid back, but is often based on financial need. These usually come from the federal and state levels of government, but sometimes from the school itself.

- Loans: Money you can borrow from different sources (e.g. Federal Perkins Loan), but that has to be paid back with interest. One key factor to consider when looking at loans is the interest rate. The lower it is the better, but also make sure to understand all the terms of the loan, including the amount of time you have to pay it back and when you have to start making payments.

  Another key fact to know about loans is whether they are subsidized or unsubsidized. Subsidized loans, usually available through the government, are better than unsubsidized ones, because it means that the government is paying the interest on your loan while you're in school—making the overall cost of the loan cheaper for you. You don't have to start paying interest on a subsidized loan until after school. Unsubsidized loans start accruing interest, which you have to pay, as soon as you take out the loan.

- Work-Study: A program that provides part-time jobs to students with financial need to help earn money for college. Basically, if you qualify, the federal government will pay a part of your wages for the work

---

14   www.fastweb.com

you do so that you can use that money to pay for college. These jobs are often on campus, and "work-study students" are attractive to employers because they only have to pay a part of your wages; the government covers the other part.

Key Terms:

Expected Family Contribution (EFC)

Your EFC may be the single most important number when it comes to affording college. EFC is basically the amount of money that the federal government thinks your family should be able to contribute toward your college education. The number is calculated when you complete your FAFSA (see below), using a special formula and taking into account your family's financial situation. Most students are considered "dependent" when determining their EFC, so it takes into account parent information like income, number of children (including the number that will be in college at same time), taxes, etc. Your EFC is the same regardless of school.

Many people are surprised by their EFC because what the government says you *should* be able to afford and what you *realistically* can afford are two very different numbers.

Free Application for Federal Student Aid (aka FAFSA)

This is the application that you need to fill out *every year* in order to be eligible for federal need-based financial aid, including loans. Most schools also require you to complete a FAFSA to qualify for any of their "need-based" aid. By filling out the FAFSA, you'll receive your EFC, which is used to determine how much "need-based" aid you qualify for.

The FAFSA becomes available on October 1 every year, and is open until June 30. A lot of aid is available on a first-come, first-served basis, so file as early as possible once it become available. I recommend completing your FAFSA at the same time that you do your college applications. Also, some states and schools have priority deadlines for filling out the FAFSA. To submit your FAFSA, you'll need your family's "prior-prior year" tax returns. For instance, if you're applying for Fall 2019, you'll use your family's 2017 tax returns.

Even if you don't think that your family will qualify for need-based aid, fill it out! There's nothing worse than potentially missing out on free money, simply because you didn't apply.

Cost of Attendance (COA)

The overall cost of attending a specific school includes tuition, fees, books, housing, meals, transportation, personal fees, etc. Every school's financial aid office is required to post estimated student budgets. Your actual costs can differ depending on the choices that you make about living expenses, meal plans, books, personal expenses, etc. However, this gives you a pretty good estimate on how much it costs to go to school.

In Division I, schools are allowed to provide student-athletes with scholarships that cover the full cost of attendance. This means that they can pay all of your regular school costs (tuition, books, room/board), *plus* provide an additional cash stipend to cover these additional personal expenses—up to the school's published COA. This is truly the only way in which someone has a full-ride scholarship. The stipend amount differs between each school, and is determined by the school's financial aid office. Coaches are now using these differences in cash stipends as a recruiting tool.

Be aware that just because DI schools *can* provide student-athletes with COA scholarships, many do not have the budget to do so. Some schools require that student-athletes in certain sports get full COA scholarships (mostly football and basketball). However, the reality is that even with the change in Division I financial aid rules, most Division I student-athletes are still not on "full" scholarships. Under Division II rules, COA scholarships are not allowed. Division II is only allowed to award scholarships up to an amount called a "grant-in-aid."

Grant in Aid (GIA)

This is an NCAA term that refers to the full cost for tuition, required fees, books, room, and board. It does not include all of the items in a school's costs of attendance, such as transportation or personal expenses. In Division II, schools cannot provide an added stipend to cover those additional costs that make up the full cost of attendance, and athletic scholarships cannot exceed the cost of a grant in aid.

So, if you are getting the maximum allowed scholarship in Division II, it's likely that there are still going to be costs that you are responsible for, because a school is only allowed to award up to the GIA amount. That's why, before you commit to a school (which we'll get to in the next chapter), you need to understand what you are and aren't getting financially. Most Division II student-athletes are only on partial scholarships, so you and your family need to understand what your costs will be at a school and how you can cover those expenses.

FAFSA4caster

An online calculator tool, FAFSA4caster[15] helps you get an early estimate of your EFC and how much federal aid you might qualify for. Keep in mind that it won't include any need-based state or institutional aid that you might be eligible for, which might be a lot. FAFSA4caster just estimates the amount of federal aid: Pell Grant, Work-

---

15   www.fafsa.ed.gov/FAFSA/app/f4cForm

Study, and Federal Stafford Loan. The tool lets you plug in a school's COA plus any other money you might be getting (e.g. state grants, institutional grants, other scholarships), and gives you a cost worksheet. Remember, this is just an estimator tool, not an actual FAFSA application! Your actual EFC and what you qualify for might change once you file your FAFSA.

Athletic Scholarship Myths and Realities

Now that we've covered the financial aid basics, including some planning tools, let's get to the real reason you're here: athletic scholarships. The best way to fill you in on what you need to know is by debunking the four most common myths about athletic scholarships.

Myth No. 1: All college student-athletes get athletic scholarships.

Reality No. 1: Many collegiate athletes aren't on any athletic scholarship at all. Division III doesn't even offer athletic scholarships. The reality is that plenty of collegiate student-athletes aren't on an athletic scholarship, and have to fund their college education through other sources: non-athletic scholarships, grants, work-study, loans, etc. That's why it's so important to do the following:

- File your FAFSA as close as possible to October 1

- Research and apply for outside scholarship opportunities

- Work hard in the classroom so that you can have an opportunity to qualify for merit-based (aka academic) aid

Myth No. 2: A "full ride" means a "free ride."

Reality No. 2: Remember the terms "COA" and "GIA"? If not, revisit them in the Key Terms section of this chapter. The reality is that the only true full ride is for those limited number of Division I students-athletes who get full cost-of-attendance scholarships. For most scholarship athletes, there are out-of-pocket costs that you are going to need to cover. That's why it's so important to understand exactly what you're getting when you are offered an athletic scholarship. Ask the coach if you can meet with someone from the school's financial aid office to review your EFC and potential aid package. Ask questions and make sure that you understand each of the sources of aid that are in your package. If any of the aid needs to be paid back (i.e. loans), make sure that you know the requirements.

Myth No. 3: An athletic scholarship is a four-year guarantee.

Reality No. 3: There are no guarantees in life. Before you sign on for an athletic scholarship, you need to make sure that you understand the terms and conditions of the award. In Division I, some schools award four-year scholarships, but not all currently do. Division II and NAIA schools are only allowed to make one-year awards. This means that at the end of the year, the coach can decide to reduce, increase, or not renew your scholarship *for any reason*, including your athletic performance. However, if you signed a four-year scholarship agreement at a Division I school, the coach cannot reduce or cancel your scholarship during those four years for athletics reasons like poor performance, or for injury or illness.

Four-year awards are a big topic right now in college athletics, so you might see a change in the rules in the near future.

You should also be aware of the specific reasons that a coach (both DI and DII) can cancel or reduce your scholarship during the year. Basically, it is only if you are legitimately messing up by doing one or more of the following:

- You make yourself ineligible by not making grades
- You fraudulently misrepresent yourself (e.g. you lie on an application)
- You engage in serious misconduct at the school
- You voluntarily leave the team
- You violate a team, department, or university rule

NCAA rules don't allow a coach to cancel or reduce your scholarship during the year for poor performance, injury, or illness. The key is to read over an athletic scholarship agreement before signing it. Ask for a copy of the team rules so that there are no unwelcome surprises down the line!

Myth No. 4: If I want an athletic scholarship, I have to focus on Division I.

Reality No. 4: By this point, hopefully you've already recognized that this is a myth! If your goal is to play in college and get a scholarship, then you shouldn't limit yourself to just Division I. Between Divisions I, II, and the NAIA, there are plenty of athletic scholarship opportunities to explore. And remember, just because DIII doesn't offer *athletic* scholarships doesn't mean that it offers *no* scholarships. Division III is the largest division and it's possible to get a great aid package that could rival any athletic scholarship.

Now that we've got financial aid and athletic scholarships down, let's move on to our last topic: committing.

13. KNOW: What It Means to Commit

If there's one thing that gets all kinds of hype in the recruiting process, it's signing day. Everyone gets excited about "making it official," tweeting out where they're going with a picture of them in the college's hat or t-shirt. But even before the official signing day arrives, there are other ways in which recruits commit to schools. So, before you make a commitment, make sure that you know what it means.

Types of Commitments

When you get down to it, there are two main ways to commit: 1) unofficially through a verbal agreement, and 2) officially with a written offer. Here's the lowdown on both.

Verbal Commitment:

NCAA rules don't allow recruits to officially sign any type of commitment until their senior year of high school. However, that doesn't stop coaches and recruits from committing to one another before then—sometimes well before then! In some sports, it's not uncommon for recruits to "verbal" (verbally commit) during their sophomore year. As you've learned, there are many rules regarding the timing and type of contact that a coach can have with a recruit. However, there are no rules (at least not just yet) about when a recruit can and can't verbally commit. You can verbal at any time and at any age.

So, what does this mean? When a coach makes a verbal commitment to you, it means that they plan to offer you some sort of written commitment, typically a scholarship. When *you* verbal, it's like telling a coach that when the time comes, you'll officially accept their offer and intend to go to school there.

Now, not all verbals are created equal; in fact, there are two levels of verbal commitments:

1. Soft Verbal – When you commit to a school but you're still talking to other coaches and visiting other schools. It's like telling a coach, "You're my number one right now, and if everything stays the same, I'm playing for you. But, I'm still keeping my options open."

2. Hard Verbal – When you commit to a school and stop contact with other coaches. It's like telling a coach, "I'm 100%, and I'm not even looking at anyone else!" The reality is that when most people verbal, this is what they mean.

Regardless of whether we're talking about a "soft" or "hard" verbal, remember that *all* verbals are non-binding, unofficial agreements. This means that at the end of the day, neither of you are officially obligated to do anything. You can change your mind about them, and they can change their mind about you—for any reason and at any time. You might ask, "Then what's the point?"

The point of a verbal commitment is that it gives both you and the coach some level of assurance that you want them and they want you. This of course doesn't mean that it's a done deal! While there are plenty of coaches and recruits who honor their word, the reality is that both coaches and recruits change their minds all the time. For that reason, some coaches might not even let you verbally commit at an early age, not necessarily because they don't want you, but because they know it's too early for either of you to be making that sort of commitment. Too many things can happen: coaching change, injury, better recruits come along, you get a better offer from another coach, etc. I'm not saying that it's a bad idea to verbally commit, and I'm not saying that coaches who allow early commitments aren't people of their word. All I'm advising is that you proceed with caution and don't be caught off guard.

Written Commitment:

Just like with verbals, there are different ways through which you can officially commit to a school in writing. And, just like with verbals, you need to know what each of them means before you sign.

- National Letter of Intent (NLI) – Used only in Divisions I and II, the NLI is the most well-known form of commitment. It officially binds you to the school and them to you. The school is required to provide you with an athletic scholarship for at least one year. You are required to attend that school for at least one year. If you choose to go to a different NCAA school other than where you signed, you can't compete your first year. That's the standard penalty. Additionally, once you sign a NLI, coaches from other DI or DII schools are supposed to stop trying to recruit you and you shouldn't be talking to them.

The two biggest misconceptions about the NLI are:

- An NLI equals a full ride
- An NLI is a binding agreement with the coach

Both of these are wrong. You know number one is not true based on Chapter 12. An NLI requires *some* amount of athletic scholarship, but it certainly does not mean a full ride. Number two is wrong because an NLI is an agreement between you and the school, not you and the coach. If the coach changes schools, which can always happen, you're still tied to the school that you signed with. Maybe the school will let you out of the NLI agreement if that happens, but maybe not. Are you comfortable with that?

- Scholarship Offer – Similar to an NLI minus the NLI part. A scholarship offer is binding on the school, but there's technically nothing binding on your end. If you decide to go elsewhere, because of a coaching change or for any other reason, there's no one-year penalty like with the NLI, nor is there a recruiting ban. Basically, for you, a scholarship offer is a lower risk version of the NLI.

  For the coach, this isn't as great an option because it does not come with a recruiting ban or other penalty. A coach would rather "lock it in" with an NLI. That being said, if you're not comfortable with the terms of an NLI, and you feel strongly that you're a "can't lose" recruit to the coach, negotiate for a scholarship-only option. If you decide to go that route, always proceed with caution in the negotiation game. If you're not as valuable to the coach as you think you are, they could very easily say "better luck elsewhere."

- Commitment Letter – Some schools will offer an institutional or conference letter of intent, committing themselves to you. However, there is no scholarship attached and no binding obligation on your end. If it's a conference letter of intent, it might include a conference recruiting ban as well as a penalty if you opt out and instead attend a conference rival.

- Celebratory Athletics Signing Form – This is strictly a Division III commitment letter. It is non-binding on both sides, and a coach can't send it to you until you've officially been accepted to the school. Regardless of the fact that it's non-binding, this is a good way to formalize your commitment to one another on the DIII level.

- NAIA Commitments – The NAIA does not have a letter of intent program. Schools (and NAIA conferences) are allowed to make their own commitment programs. These are non-binding agreements for you and they may or may not include offers of athletics aid. Unless you're signing a conference letter of intent, where there may be a penalty for choosing to go to a conference rival, in general there are no penalties for you. Unlike in the NCAA, NAIA rules don't limit when a recruit can sign a written offer, so you can sign whenever you feel is right for you.

There's one other thing that I want to clarify: I'm not saying that some of these types of commitments are better than others simply because they are non-binding on you. I strongly believe that you should only sign if you fully intend to honor the agreement. At the end of the day, you need to protect yourself by making sure that you understand what you're signing and by doing what's right for you.

Signing Day

Technically, "National Signing Day" refers to the first day of the signing period in NCAA football. However, in all NCAA Division I and II sports, there are different signing periods when recruits can officially sign commitment letters with schools. The first day of the signing period for the sport is known as "signing day." Many high schools have signing ceremonies for their students, where they'll officially sign their commitment letters wearing a shirt or hat from their college.

Tip

Sometimes, there are certain reasons why a coach can't use an NLI, namely for some transfer students. NLI rules only allow you to sign one valid NLI, so it might be the case that some transfers aren't even eligible to sign an NLI and a scholarship offer is the only option.

Other Key Terms to Know

Redshirt:

Under NCAA rules, a student-athlete is allowed to compete for four seasons; however, those four seasons can be stretched out over five years (or 10 full-time semesters in Division II). When a student-athlete's career stretches out over five years, it's because they "redshirted" a season. A redshirt is a full member of the team and can practice and receive aid, but they cannot compete in any outside competition during that particular season. By redshirting, they are extending their career to five years by "saving" a season. Usually, this is done during a student-athlete's freshman year to allow them to develop for an extra year before competing, or because there's a more senior member of the team ahead of them in their position.

Oversigning:

This is traditionally more of an issue with Division I BCS football programs, though you'll find stories of it happening in Division I baseball, basketball, and probably a few other sports. At the end of the day, this is *not* something I'd call commonplace. In general, oversigning is looked down upon, but it is something to be aware of in some Division I sports.

Oversigning occurs when a coach signs more recruits to scholarships than they have to give. For example, NCAA rules might only allow a coach to have 13 scholarship athletes on the team. Let's say there are nine returners with scholarships, which means only four scholarships are available. The coach then sends out six scholarship offers. If more than four recruits accept, that's oversigning.

Why would a coach do that? Knowing that not all offers will be accepted or otherwise pan out, NCAA rules do not prohibit a coach from offering more scholarships than they have available in a given recruiting cycle. Some recruits might choose to go elsewhere and not accept the offer, others might end up not meeting eligibility requirements, nor get accepted into the school. A different, less well-intentioned reason why a coach might oversign is because they are trying to stockpile recruits in order to prevent them from signing with a rival. No matter what the reason, if a coach gets into a bind, they have to make room to meet their scholarship limit somehow, and that's where oversigning gets its bad reputation.

One solution to this is something called grayshirting.

Grayshirting:

Grayshirting (again, typically only used in football), is when a recruit delays their college enrollment—usually by one semester, but up to a year. They will either not enroll in school at all, or will enroll as a part-time student (most common) and pay their own way for that/those term(s). During that time, they are not allowed to be involved with the team. Then, when they enroll as a full-time student, they can officially join the team with a scholarship. By delaying enrollment, the coach is able to avoid an oversigning situation because the recruit is now part of next year's recruiting class, where theoretically there's room in terms of the scholarship limit. The recruit still maintains full access to their five years of eligibility.

A Final Word on Commitments

Keep in mind that athletic commitments are not offers or guarantees of admission to the school. I'd like to think that a coach *shouldn't* be offering you any sort of commitment unless they know that you have a strong case for getting into the school, but that's not always the case. In fact, these offers become null and void if you don't get into the school. They're also not a guarantee that you're meeting NCAA eligibility requirements. Bottom line: look out for *you*! Before you sign, make sure that you know where you stand in terms of admission to the school and meeting NCAA eligibility requirements.

14. KNOW: What to Do
After You Commit

One of the most critical things you can do once you've committed is to remember that committing is just the first step into your college career—it's not the end of your athletic journey. So, treat it that way. Should you celebrate your commitment? Absolutely, because it's a big deal! However, realize that there are several key things you can do after you've committed to increase your chances of a successful transition from high school to college:

- Stay focused in the classroom; you've put in too much work up to this point to start letting your grades slip now. Remember, it's a very real possibility that if you don't meet a certain academic level in your senior year, your admission status could be in danger and it could even negatively impact your NCAA eligibility standing. Resist the temptation of "senioritis" and power through.

- Start working on improving your study habits and time management skills. The jump from high school-level work to college-level work is usually a big one for most people. The biggest difference tends to be the amount of time spent on your sport and the amount of time you need to spend on your studies in order to perform well. As a student-athlete, you own less of your time than other students. You've got practice, games, weights, conditioning, team travel, and rehab—and you can't set the schedule for these. It's almost guaranteed that during your season, at least 20 hours of how your

time is spent each week will be dictated by someone else (and that doesn't include *everything* you'll
have to do with the team). So, you need to become
a master at managing your time. You may have
required study hall sessions once you get to college,
but you still need to take responsibility for your
time.

Use your remaining time in high school, as well
as the summer before college, to hone your time
management skills. Find a system that works for
you, whether that's using a planner or scheduling
your time using your phone. Also, start getting
comfortable with the idea that you might have to
say no to certain things. Half the battle with time
management is prioritizing and learning when to
say "yes" and when to say "no."

- Reconnect with the coach to talk about what kinds
  of academic support exist for student-athletes. If
  your goal is to do well academically in college, then
  make sure that you know what your school offers
  in terms of support. It's better to be aware of and
  use these resources from the beginning than to
  wait until you're struggling. That being said, if you
  get into your first semester or quarter and are having trouble, don't be too proud to ask for help. For
  some students, college is the first time that they've
  struggled academically. You might feel embarrassed
  to admit that you need help, but unless you com-
  municate with the coach or an academic advisor,
  they can't get you the help that you might need.

- Stay on the straight and narrow in your personal
  life (this includes your presence online). I men-
  tioned this earlier in the book: coaches pay attention to what you do off the field, and negative

off-field antics can certainly impact your athletic career. This is especially important if your commitment isn't "official" yet. Many coaches monitor recruit's social media feeds, and if they see something that makes them pause, they might just hit the pause button on your recruitment! So, make sure that your off-field behavior stays clean.

- Commit to continuing to improve your game. There's that old adage: if you're not getting better, you're getting worse. While you're certainly entitled to take a breather and revel in your future collegiate career, don't completely rest on your laurels. Make sure that you're still honing your skills because your future teammates and opponents are definitely working on theirs.

- Stay (or become) strong, fit, and healthy. The difference between high school and college is serious: players are bigger, faster, and stronger. The toll on your body from the volume of work that you're doing in practice, weights, and competitions is likely more than you've experienced before. For that reason, it's not uncommon for freshmen to get injured during their first year. The body either just gets so exhausted that it's susceptible to injuries, or it can't yet handle the physicality of college-level play. If you want to not only limit your chances of injury but also make an impact right away, follow the summer fitness program that your coach sends you. Let's be honest: many players don't do it or only do so halfway. If you commit to the program, you're giving yourself a head start on the competition—and maybe even your future teammates.

So on that note, we've made it all the way through the recruiting process from beginning to end, and even covered what to do after you've committed. Now's when the rubber meets the road; be confident in yourself, your abilities, and your dreams. Good luck and go make it happen...

Recruit You!

Appendix

Division I Sliding Scale*

Combined SAT score = reading + math subscores

ACT sum score = English+math+reading+science subscores

Core GPA	SAT	ACT				
3.55+	400	37		2.7	740	61
3.525	410	38		2.675	750	61
3.5	420	39		2.65	760	62
3.475	430	40		2.625	770	63
3.45	440	41		2.6	780	64
3.425	450	41		2.575	790	65
3.4	460	42		2.55	800	66
3.375	470	42		2.525	810	67
3.35	480	43		2.5	820	68
3.325	490	44		2.475	830	69
3.3	500	44		2.45	840	70
3.275	510	45		2.425	850	70
3.25	520	46		2.4	860	71
3.225	530	46		2.375	870	72
3.2	540	47		2.35	880	73
3.175	550	47		2.325	890	74
3.15	560	48		2.3	900	75
3.125	570	49		**Below 2.3 = Academic Redshirt**		
3.1	580	49		2.299	910	76
3.075	590	50		2.275	910	76
3.05	600	50		2.25	920	77
3.025	610	51		2.225	930	78
3	620	52		2.2	940	79
2.975	630	52		2.175	950	80
2.95	640	53		2.15	960	81
2.925	650	53		2.125	970	82
2.9	660	54		2.1	980	83
2.875	670	55		2.075	990	84
2.85	680	56		2.05	1000	85
2.825	690	56		2.025	1010	86
2.8	700	57		2.00	1020	86
2.775	710	58				
2.75	720	59				
2.725	730	60				

Remember: The scale is based on the "old" SAT model so if you took the SAT on or after March 2016, you must convert your score into an equivalent "old" score using the SAT Score Converter found on the College Board's website

*http://www.ncaa.org/student-athletes/future/test-scores

DII Qualifier after August 1, 2018*

Combined SAT score = reading + math subscores
ACT sum score = English+math+reading+science subscores

Core GPA	SAT	ACT				
3.300+	400	37		2.6	680	56
3.275	410	38		2.575	690	56
3.25	420	39		2.55	700	57
3.225	430	40		2.525	710	58
3.2	440	41		2.5	720	59
3.175	450	41		2.475	730	59
3.15	460	42		2.45	740	60
3.125	470	42		2.425	750	61
3.1	480	43		2.4	760	62
3.075	490	44		2.375	770	63
3.05	500	44		2.35	780	64
3.025	510	45		2.325	790	65
3	520	46		2.3	800	66
2.975	530	46		2.275	810	67
2.95	540	47		2.25	820	68
2.925	550	47		2.225	830	69
2.9	560	48		2.2	840+	70+
2.875	570	49				
2.85	580	49				
2.825	590	50				
2.8	600	50				
2.775	610	51				
2.75	620	52				
2.725	630	52				
2.7	640	53				
2.675	650	53				
2.65	660	54				
2.625	670	55				

Remember: The scale is based on the "old" SAT model so if you took the SAT on or after March 2016, you must convert your score into an equivalent "old" score using the SAT Score Converter found on the College Board's website

*http://www.ncaa.org/student-athletes/future/test-scores

DII Partial Qualifier after August 1, 2018*

Combined SAT score = reading + math subscores

ACT sum score = English+math+reading+science subscores

Core GPA	SAT	ACT				
3.050+	400	37		2.4	660	54
3.025	410	38		2.375	670	55
3	420	39		2.35	680	56
2.975	430	40		2.325	690	56
2.95	440	41		2.3	700	57
2.925	450	41		2.275	710	58
2.9	460	42		2.25	720	59
2.875	470	42		2.225	730	60
2.85	480	43		2.2	740	61
2.825	490	44		2.175	750	61
2.8	500	44		2.15	760	62
2.775	510	45		2.125	770	63
2.75	520	46		2.1	780	64
2.725	530	46		2.075	790	65
2.7	540	47		2.05	800	66
2.675	550	47		2.025	810	67
2.65	560	48		2	820+	68+
2.625	570	49				
2.6	580	49				
2.575	590	50				
2.55	600	50				
2.525	610	51				
2.5	620	52				
2.475	630	52				
2.45	640	53				
2.425	650	53				

Remember: The scale is based on the "old" SAT model so if you took the SAT on or after March 2016, you must convert your score into an equivalent "old" score using the SAT Score Converter found on the College Board's website

*http://www.ncaa.org/student-athletes/future/test-scores

Division I Core-Course & GPA Worksheet

A = 4 quality points; B = 3 quality points; C = 2 quality points; D = 1 quality point

English (4 years)

Course Name	10/7	Credits	Grade	Quality Points (credits x grade)
Sample: American Literature	√	0.5/0.5	A/B	2/1.5
1.				
2.				
3.				
4.				

(The sample has two grades, one per semester. Put all credits, grades and quality points for a course on one line)

Math (3 years)

Course Name	10/7	Credits	Grade	Quality Points (credits x grade)
1.				
2.				
3.				

Natural/Physical Science (2 years)

Course Name	10/7	Credits	Grade	Quality Points (credits x grade)
1.				
2.				

Additional year of English, math, or natural/physical science (1 year)

Course Name	10/7	Credits	Grade	Quality Points (credits x grade)
1.				

Social Science (2 years)

Course Name	10/7	Credits	Grade	Quality Points (credits x grade)
1.				
2.				

Additional core courses (4 years)

Course Name	10/7	Credits	Grade	Quality Points (credits x grade)
1.				
2.				
3.				
4.				

10 core courses must be completed before the seventh semester and 7 of the 10 must be a combination of English, math or natural or physical science for competition purposes. Put a √ if course meets 10/7

Total Quality Points
Total Credits
Core-Course GPA (Total Quality Points÷Total Credits)

Division II Core-Course & GPA Worksheet

A = 4 quality points; B = 3 quality points; C = 2 quality points; D = 1 quality point

English (3 years)

Course Name	Credits	Grade	Quality Points (credits x grade)
Sample: American Literature	0.5/0.5	A/B	2/1.5
1.			
2.			
3.			

(The sample has two grades, one per semester. Put all credits, grades and quality points for a course on one line)

Math (2 years)

Course Name	Credits	Grade	Quality Points (credits x grade)
1.			
2.			

Natural/Physical Science (2 years)

Course Name	Credits	Grade	Quality Points (credits x grade)
1.			
2.			

Additional years of English, math, or natural/physical science (3 year)

Course Name	Credits	Grade	Quality Points (credits x grade)
1.			
2.			
3.			

Social Science (2 years)

Course Name	Credits	Grade	Quality Points (credits x grade)
1.			
2.			

Additional core courses (4 years)

Course Name	Credits	Grade	Quality Points (credits x grade)
1.			
2.			
3.			
4.			

Total Quality Points	
Total Credits	
Core-Course GPA (Total Quality Points÷Total Credits)	

Goal Setting

My goal is:

_____

Goal Setting

My goal is:

_____

Priorities List

ATHLETIC	ACADEMIC	OTHER

Priorities List

ATHLETIC	ACADEMIC	OTHER

Shortlist

College	Division	Eligible (Y/N)	Admissible (Y/N)	Coach	Contact Info
1					
2					
3					
4					
5					
6					
7					
8					

9										
10										
11										
12										
13										
14										
15										
16										
17										
18										
19										
20										

Shortlist

College	Division	Eligible (Y/N)	Admissible (Y/N)	Coach	Contact Info
1					
2					
3					
4					
5					
6					
7					
8					

9	10	11	12	13	14	15	16	17	18	19	20

DIVISION I FOOTBALL RECRUITING ACTIVITY RULES

Recruiting Activity	Fresh./Soph. Year	Junior Year	Senior Year
Non-Athletic Recruiting Material*	Permitted – can send anytime	Permitted	Permitted
Athletically-Related Recruiting Material	Prohibited	Permitted starting Sept. 1 of junior year	Permitted
Electronic Correspondence (emails, texts, etc.)	Prohibited	Permitted starting Sept. 1 of junior year	Permitted
Phone Calls**	Prohibited	Prohibited except for one call between April 15–May 31	Permitted (one call per week after Sept. 1 of senior year); unlimited during contact period
Off-Campus Contact	Prohibited	Prohibited	Permitted starting July 1 after junior year (only during contact periods)
Official Visits	Prohibited	Permitted only during the time period between April 1st through the Sunday before the last Wednesday in June (confusing huh?!)	Permitted starting September 1st of senior year; one visit limit per school, with a max. of five total official visits to DI schools
Unofficial Visits	Permitted (unlimited) except during dead period	Permitted (unlimited) except during dead period	Permitted (unlimited) except during dead period
Evaluations	Permitted	Permitted	Permitted

*recruiting questionnaires; camp information/invitations; generic admissions information; NCAA eligibility guides

**Even if NCAA rules do not allow the coach to email, text or call you, you can email, text or call the coach at any time. Know they cannot respond; however, if the coach picks up their phone when you call, they are allowed to talk with you.

DIVISION I MEN'S BASKETBALL RECRUITING ACTIVITY RULES

Recruiting Activity	Fresh./Soph. Year	Junior Year	Senior Year
Non-Athletic Recruiting Material*	Permitted – can send anytime	Permitted – can send anytime	Permitted – can send anytime
Athletically-Related Recruiting Material	Prohibited	Permitted starting June 15 after sophomore year	Permitted
Electronic Correspondence (emails, texts, etc.)**	Prohibited	Permitted starting June 15 after sophomore year (unlimited)	Permitted
Phone Calls**	Prohibited	Permitted starting June 15 after sophomore year (unlimited)	Permitted
Off-Campus Contact	Prohibited	Permitted starting first day of classes of junior year	Permitted
Official Visits	Prohibited	Permitted starting Aug. 1 of junior year; 1 visit limit per school with a max. of 5 total official visits to DI schools	Permitted. Get a new set of 5 total D1 visits with 1 visit limit per school.
Unofficial Visits	Prohibited if any athletics involvement prior to Aug 1 of sophomore year.	Permitted (unlimited) except during dead periods and during July	Permitted (unlimited) except during dead periods and during July
Evaluations	Permitted	Permitted	Permitted

*Recruiting questionnaires; camp information/invitations; generic admissions information; NCAA eligibility guides

**Even if NCAA rules do not allow the coach to email, text or call you, you can email, text or call the coach at any time. Know they cannot respond; however, if the coach picks up their phone when you call, they are allowed to talk with you.

DIVISION I WOMEN'S BASKETBALL RECRUITING ACTIVITY RULES

Recruiting Activity	Fresh./Soph. Year	Junior Year	Senior Year
Non-Athletic Recruiting Material*	Permitted – can send anytime	Permitted – can send anytime	Permitted – can send anytime
Athletically-Related Recruiting Material	Prohibited	Permitted starting Sept. 1 of junior year	Permitted
Electronic Correspondence (emails, texts, etc.)	Prohibited	Permitted starting Sept. 1 of junior year (unlimited)	Permitted
Phone Calls	Prohibited	Permitted starting Sept. 1 of junior year (unlimited)	Permitted
Off-Campus Contact	Prohibited	Permitted starting March 1 of junior year.	Permitted
Official Visits	Prohibited	Permitted starting the Thursday following the NCAA women's basketball championship game; 1 visit limit per school with a max. of 5 total official visits to DI schools	Permitted, but only 1 visit limit per school with a max. of 5 total official visits to DI schools
Unofficial Visits	Permitted (unlimited) except during dead periods and during the July evaluation period	Permitted (unlimited) except during dead periods and during the July evaluation period	Permitted (unlimited) except during dead periods and during the July evaluation period
Evaluations	Permitted	Permitted	Permitted

*Recruiting questionnaires; camp information/invitations; generic admissions information; NCAA eligibility guides

**Even if NCAA rules do not allow the coach to email, text or call you, you can email, text or call the coach at any time. Know they cannot respond; however, if the coach picks up their phone when you call, they are allowed to talk with you.

DIVISION I BASEBALL RECRUITING ACTIVITY RULES

Recruiting Activity	Fresh./Soph. Year	Junior Year	Senior Year
Non-Athletic Recruiting Material*	Permitted – can send anytime	Permitted	Permitted
Athletically-Related Recruiting Material	Prohibited	Permitted starting Sept. 1 of juior year	Permitted
Electronic Correspondence (emails, texts, etc.)**	Prohibited	Permitted starting Sept. 1 of juior year	Permitted
Phone Calls**	Prohibited	Permitted starting Sept. 1 of juior year	Permitted
Off-Campus Contact	Prohibited	Prohibited	Permitted starting July 1st after junior year
Official Visits	Prohibited	Permitted starting Sept. 1 of juior year	Permitted
Unofficial Visits	Prohibited if any athletics involvement (see below)	Permitted starting Sept. 1 of juior year	Permitted (unlimited) except during dead periods
Evaluations	Permitted	Permitted	Permitted

*Recruiting questionnaires; camp information/invitations; generic admissions information; NCAA eligibility guides

**Even if NCAA rules do not allow the coach to email, text or call you, you can email, text or call the coach at any time. Know they can't respond; however, if the coach picks up their phone when you call, they are allowed to talk with you.

123

DIVISION I LACROSSE & SOFTBALL RECRUITING ACTIVITY RULES

Recruiting Activity	Fresh./Soph. Year	Junior Year	Senior Year
Non-Athletic Recruiting Material*	Permitted – can send anytime	Permitted	Permitted
Athletically-Related Recruiting Material	Prohibited	Permitted starting Sept. 1 of junior year	Permitted
Electronic Correspondence (emails, texts, etc.)**	Prohibited	Permitted starting Sept. 1 of junior year	Permitted
Phone Calls** (Both Incoming & Outgoing)	Prohibited	Permitted starting Sept. 1 of junior year	Permitted
Off-Campus Contact	Prohibited	Permitted starting Sept. 1 of junior year. Contact restricted to recruit's high school or home during junior year in Lacrosse/Softball.	Permitted
Official Visits	Prohibited	Permitted starting Sept. 1 of junior year	Permitted
Unofficial Visits	Prohibited if any athletics involvement (see below)	Permitted starting Sept. 1 of junior year. Cannot take place during dead periods.	Permitted (unlimited) except during dead periods

*Recruiting questionnaires; camp information/invitations; generic admissions information; NCAA eligibility guides

**Even if NCAA rules do not allow the coach to email, text or call you, you can email, text or call the coach at any time. Just know they can't actually talk to you or respond until the dates above.

DI Lacrosse & Softball have rules that restrict any communication or contact between recruits & coaches until September 1st of junior year. Unlike some sports where recruits can speak with a coach who picks up the phone if called, Lacrosse and Softball coaches cannot have any contact with recruits whatsoever, regardless of who initiated it, until September 1 of junior year.

Unofficial visits with athletics involvement are prohibited prior to Sept. 1 of junior year. You can, and should, visit schools before junior year, but the coach or athletics department cannot be involved in any way until that date. Also, effective 8/1/18, official visits can now start Sept 1st of junior year.

125

DIVISION I ALL OTHER SPORTS RECRUITING ACTIVITY RULES

Recruiting Activity	Fresh./Soph. Year	Junior Year	Senior Year
Non-Athletic Recruiting Material*	Permitted – can send anytime	Permitted	Permitted
Athletically-Related Recruiting Material	Prohibited except for M. Hockey – Jan 1 of soph. year	Permitted in all sports starting June 15 after sophomore year	Permitted
Electronic Correspondence (emails, texts, etc.)**	Prohibited except for M. Hockey – Jan 1 of soph. year	Permitted in all sports starting June 15 after sophomore year	Permitted
Phone Calls**	Prohibited except for M. Hockey, which can make unlimited calls starting Jan. 1 of soph. year	Permitted in all sports starting June 15 after sophomore year	Permitted
Off-Campus Contact	Prohibited	Permitted starting August 1st before juinor year	Permitted
Official Visits	Prohibited	Permitted starting August 1st before juinor year	Permitted starting on 1st day of classes of senior year. 1 visit limit per school with max. of 5 total official visits to DI schools.

Unofficial Visits	Prohibited if any athletics involvement (see below) EXCEPT M. Hockey which allows starting Jan 1 of soph. year	Permitted starting August 1st before junior year EXCEPT M. Hockey which allows in soph. year	Permitted (unlimited) except during dead periods
Evaluations	Permitted	Permitted	Permitted

*Recruiting questionnaires; camp information/invitations; generic admissions information; NCAA eligibility guides

**Even if NCAA rules do not allow the coach to email, text or call you, you can email, text or call the coach at any time. Just know they can't actually talk to you or respond until the dates above.

Unofficial visits with athletics involvement are prohibited prior to Sept. 1 of junior year. You can, and should, visit schools before junior year, but the coach or athletics department cannot be involved in any way until that date. Also, effective 8/1/18, official visits can now start Sept 1st of junior year.

DIVISION II ALL SPORTS RECRUITING ACTIVITY RULES

Recruiting Activity	Fresh./Soph. Year	Junior Year	Senior Year
Non-Athletic Recruiting Material*	Permitted – can send anytime	Permitted	Permitted
Athletically-Related Recruiting Material	Prohibited	Permitted starting June 15 after sophomore year	Permitted
Electronic Correspondence (emails, texts, etc.)**	Prohibited	Permitted starting June 15 after sophomore year (unlimited)	Permitted
Phone Calls**	Prohibited	Permitted starting June 15 after sophomore year (unlimited)	Permitted
Off-Campus Contact	Prohibited	Permitted starting June 15 after sophomore year (unlimited)	Permitted
Official Visits	Prohibited	Permitted starting June 15 after sophomore year; 1 visit limit per school, but no limit on total number	Permitted, but only 1 visit per school
Unofficial Visits	Permitted (unlimited) except during dead periods	Permitted (unlimited) except during dead periods	Permitted (unlimited) except during dead periods
Evaluations	Permitted	Permitted	Permitted

*Recruiting questionnaires; camp information/invitations; generic admissions information; NCAA eligibility guides

**Even if NCAA rules do not allow the coach to email, text or call you, you can email, text or call the coach at any time. Know they cannot respond; however, if the coach picks up their phone when you call, they allowed to talk with you.

DIVISION III ALL SPORTS RECRUITING ACTIVITY RULES

Recruiting Activity	Fresh./Soph. Year	Junior Year	Senior Year
Non-Athletic Recruiting Material*	No restrictions – coaches can send any type of printed recruiting material at any time	Permitted	Permitted
Athletically-Related Recruiting Material	No restrictions – coaches can send any type of printed recruiting material at any time	Permitted	Permitted
Electronic Correspondence (emails, texts, etc.)	No restrictions – coaches can initiate and respond to emails, texts, etc. at any time	Permitted	Permitted
Phone Calls	No restrictions – coaches can initiate and return phone calls at any time	Permitted	Permitted
Off-Campus Contact	Prohibited	Permitted after the end of sophomore year	Permitted
Official Visits	Prohibited	Permitted starting Jan. 1 of junior year; only one visit per school	Permitted, but only one visit per school
Unofficial Visits	Permitted	Permitted	Permitted
Evaluations	Permitted	Permitted	Permitted

*Recruiting questionnaires; camp information/invitations; generic admissions information; NCAA eligibility guides

Sample Introductory Email:

Subject Line: 2019 Power Forward - Sally Smith

Dear Coach Johnson,

My name is Sally Smith. I am a 2019 recruit from Nowhereville, CA. I wanted to introduce myself because I am interested in playing basketball for you at Gold Medal University.

I am a 6'2" power forward. Last season I earned All-District Honors averaging 18.9 points per game and 9.5 rebounds. As a student, I have a 3.5 GPA and scored a 1630 on the SAT. I have listed my coach and team information below.

I am interested in playing at Gold Medal University because you have a strong program, and I think my style of play fits well with your team. Also, academics is important to me and Gold Medal University has a good biology program.

I have attached my transcript and test scores. I have also included a link to my video highlights and a copy of my team's upcoming regular season schedule. I encourage you to speak with my coaches about me, and hope you can see me play this season.

Thank you,

Sally Smith, 2019

sallysmith@hoops.com

555-555-5555

www.sallysmithvideo.com

[Attach a document labeled "Team & Coach Info" that includes the below information.]

High School:

Nowhereville High School, #5

Coach: John Hoops

777-777-777; jhoops@highschool.edu

Club Team:

Nowhereville Swoosh, #12

Coach: Jane Ball

333-333-3333; jball@swoosh.com

Sample Mid-Year Update Email:

Subject Line: 2019 Power Forward - Sally Smith

Hi Coach Johnson,

This is Sally Smith, 2019 recruit from Nowhereville, MA. Congratulations on a great season. I was able to see the team play when you were in Boston in February.

My high school team did well this season winning conference. I ended the season averaging 22.5 points per game and 7.5 rebounds. I will be playing with my club team, Nowhereville Swoosh, this summer. I have attached a copy of my travel schedule for the summer and some updated highlights from the season. I also included an updated transcript that shows my grades from the fall.

I encourage you to speak to my coaches about me, and hope you are able to see me play this summer.

Thank you,

Sally Smith, 2019

sallysmith@hoops.com

555-555-5555

www.sallysmithvideo.com

[Attach a document labeled "Team & Coach Info" that includes the below information.]

High School:

Nowhereville High School, #5

Coach: John Hoops

777-777-777; jhoops@highschool.edu

Club Team:

Nowhereville Swoosh, #12

Coach: Jane Ball

333-333-3333; jball@swoosh.com

Sample Summer Update Email

Subject Line: 2019 Power Forward - Sally Smith

Hi Coach Johnson,

This is Sally Smith, 2019 recruit from Nowhereville, MA. I know you're probably busy with summer recruiting.

Next weekend I am playing in the End of the Trail Showcase in Oregon. I am not sure if you are going to be there, but I will be playing with Nowhereville Swoosh and wearing #12. I hope you'll have a chance to see me play.

I have also attached my updated transcript with my spring grades and updated test score. I now have a 3.1 and scored 27 on the ACT.

Thank you,

Sally Smith, 2019

sallysmith@hoops.com

555-555-5555

www.sallysmithvideo.com

[Attach a document labeled "Team & Coach Info" that includes the below information.]

High School:

Nowhereville High School, #5

Coach: John Hoops

777-777-777; jhoops@highschool.edu

Club Team:

Nowhereville Swoosh, #12

Coach: Jane Ball

333-333-3333; jball@swoosh.com

Sample Introductory Phone Call Script

[Make sure to speak clearly and no matter how nervous you are, don't rush!]

Hello Coach Johnson:

My name is Roger Smith. I am a 2019 recruit. *[Pause–let the coach get their bearings].* I wanted to introduce myself. Is now a good time?*

I have been following the team, and saw that you won last week against Bronze Metal University. *[This lets the coach know you're actually interested].* I am a 6'5" outside hitter and touch 11'6". I think I could be a good fit for your team.

[Be prepared to answer some questions about yourself at this point]

I hit 0.379 and had 14 aces on the season. I'm looking for a school that I can play for where I can study business. I have a 2.8 GPA and scored a 1500 on the SATs last month.

I wanted to send you some video so you can see how I play, and I'll include a copy of my club team's schedule for the summer. Hope you have a chance to see me play.

Thank you for your time.

[It's entirely possible that at this point the coach might say thank you for the call, but that they're actually finished recruiting for their 2019 class. If that's the case, don't just say "Oh. Ok. Thank you." and then hang up. Instead, respond with something along the lines of "Well, I hope that if something changes and you need an outside hitter, that you'll keep me in mind. Thank you for your time."]

133

Athletic Resume Template

Name, Graduation Year

Email Address

Phone Number

Eligibility Center ID

[Insert Photo]

Academic Information

GPA

Test Score (highest)

High School

Intended Major

Major academic awards/accomplishments

Athletics Information/Stats

Height/Weight/Bats/Throws (if applicable)

Position

Important Stats/Personal Records

Teams

High School Team

Jersey Number (if applicable)

Coach Name & Contact Information

Club Team

Coach Name & Contact Information

Jersey Number (if applicable)

Video

Highlights: Insert Link

Full Length Game: Insert Link

Stay Up-to-Date:

In case of tweaks to recruiting rules throughout the year
and to get monthly recruiting tips & news, visit
www.recruityousports.com and
sign up for the Recruit You Newsletter!

Made in the USA
Middletown, DE
09 February 2020

84495121R00076